THE JAPANESE ART
OF SELF-ACCEPTANCE

桜梅桃李

OUBAITORI

SAORI OKADA

GODSFIELD

To those longing to bloom in their own way.

First published in Great Britain in 2026 by
Godsfield Press, an imprint of
Octopus Publishing Group Ltd
Carmelite House
50 Victoria Embankment
London EC4Y 0DZ
www.octopusbooks.co.uk

An Hachette UK Company
www.hachette.co.uk

The authorized representative in the EEA is
Hachette Ireland, 8 Castlecourt Centre,
Dublin 15, D15 XTP3, Ireland
(email: info@hbgi.ie)

Distributed in the US by Hachette Book Group
1290 Avenue of the Americas, 4th and 5th
Floors, New York, NY 10104

Distributed in Canada by Canadian Manda
Group, 664 Annette St., Toronto, Ontario,
Canada M6S 2C8

ISBN: 978-1-84181-670-8
eISBN: 978-1-84181-671-5

A CIP catalogue record for this book is available
from the British Library.

Printed and bound in China.

10 9 8 7 6 5 4 3 2 1

Commissioning Editor Louisa Johnson
Art Director Jaz Bahra
Designer Megan van Staden
Senior Editor Alex Stetter
Assistant Editor Alice Gawthrop
Picture Research Manager Jen Veall
Production Managers Lucy Carter and
Nic Jones

Images: marukopum/Shutterstock
Additional picture credits: iStock/elico-polo 187,
ioanmasay 51; Shutterstock/AQ_taro_neo 39

MIX
Paper | Supporting
responsible forestry
FSC® C016973
FSC
www.fsc.org

CONTENTS

WELCOMING OUBAITORI

MY JOURNEY TO OUBAITORI

Growing up in the busy streets of Tokyo, Japan, one of the most metropolitan areas in the world, you might think that nature is out of reach. To my surprise, I found this not to be true. Nature was closely integrated into the city, whether it was a park near my school or a quiet temple hidden among towering office buildings.

When I think back to my childhood, the first blossoms I vividly remember are the sakura, or cherry blossoms, lining the streets in the spring. My mother would pick me up from school, and my older sister and I would gaze upwards during the drive home, watching as the blossoms slowly opened day by day. These rows of trees are called sakura namiki, or avenues of cherry blossom trees, and in those moments of awe, we absorbed the beauty of nature.

Each blossom opened, flourished and then drifted to the ground in its own brief moment. Usually, it took a week or two, but sometimes it could be just a few short days because of bad weather. Even at a young age, I could feel my connection to nature in this moment. This memory is a lesson of fleeting beauty, the heart of Japan's beloved hanami tradition, or the art of flower viewing.

At the same time, my childhood experience was also shaped by time abroad – my family lived in the United States for three years and I attended an international school in Japan. This early exposure widened my view of the world but also created a focus and desire to look beyond Japan, to almost not pay attention to my Japanese roots, as it was not the 'cool' thing to be as I entered my early teenage years. I found myself pushing away the traditions and rituals that my parents, aunts, uncles and grandparents were trying to share with me.

It wasn't until I was in my twenties, after moving abroad for university, that an undeniable yearning grew inside me. I felt a tug to reconnect with the roots I had so strongly pushed away in my teen years. At that time, I was also going through a personal wellbeing journey, facing challenges rooted in perfectionism and a hyper-focus on physical appearance as a measure of self-worth, which led to a long battle with eating disorders. Despite achieving many of the societal labels of success, including getting a good job, living in New York City – one of the best cities in the world – and having financial stability, I could not shake this deep sense of emptiness and unhappiness. My internal monologue at that time was constantly filled with questions, often comparing myself to others: *Why don't I feel like I am enough? Why does happiness seem to come easier to others? How come I feel so behind?* The pressure to act as though I had everything together and appear 'perfect' was taking a toll on me.

Through patience, self-compassion and the support of my community, I went through my healing journey, where I learned to lean into my authentic, holistic self, embracing mind, body and soul. It was during this time that I reconnected with the cultural wisdom I had grown up with, where I remembered to be my true self – one that does not have to be perfect but uniquely beautiful and worthy, just as each of us is.

It was only years later, after moving to London, that I came across the phrase *ōbaitōri* – 桜梅桃李, commonly rendered in English as oubaitori. This four-character idiom reminds us that each blossom – cherry (*sakura* 桜), Japanese apricot (*ume* 梅), peach (*momo* 桃) and Japanese plum (*sumomo* 李) – has its own time to bloom, and none compares itself to the others.

Each blooms in its own season and has unique value and significance in Japanese culture. It named a truth I had been living but hadn't found words for: similar to these blossoms, we each have our own rhythm and path, none better or worse, all beautiful in their own way.

THE CONSTANT COMPARISON GAME

In today's society, the world seems to be filled with competition and comparison. The rise of social media, AI-powered tools that enhance appearances and the fast pace of living have all contributed to the persistent and ever-present shadow of comparison. Many young people today report feeling less satisfied with their lives after comparing themselves to others online – especially on social media. This is not only a challenge for younger people, it is also felt across all generations. The feelings of unworthiness I experienced in New York City in my twenties were not unique to me, but perhaps something most of us can recognize.

This constant measuring against others can dim our sense of joy and self-worth. We find ourselves asking: *Why am I not as accomplished? Why am I not as beautiful? Why am I not as well-liked?*

While some healthy comparisons can help us grow into our best selves, the current climate of unrealistic expectations creates unease, fuels stress and contributes to the rising challenges in mental wellbeing.

The antidote to this is to embrace the wisdom of oubaitori. It encourages us to release comparisons and bring the attention we all deserve back to ourselves. It is a way to give us back agency to remember that we are all uniquely unfolding in our own lives. Like the blossoms, we bloom in our own time, in our own way, and that alone is beautiful and worthy.

LESSONS FROM THE BLOSSOMS

The Japanese idiom *ōbaitōri* (桜梅桃李) celebrates four spring blossoms. We start with the cherry blossom (*sakura* 桜), followed by the Japanese apricot blossom (*ume* 梅), the peach blossom (*momo* 桃), and finally the Japanese plum blossom (*sumomo* 李). They represent four trees that bloom in spring, each with its own distinct timing, qualities and beauty.

The Japanese apricot blossoms arrive first, blooming from late January to April, often pushing through the cold winter. These brave flowers teach us resilience and strength, showing us the ability to open despite challenging conditions. Peach blossoms arrive from mid-March through April, radiating playful joy and creative spirit. Cherry blossoms follow a similar timeline, appearing from mid-March to early May. The transient but striking flowers represent the beauty of fleeting moments, impermanence and the wonder of presence. Finally, we have the Japanese plum, its blossoms opening calmly between March and April alongside the others. While the Japanese plum blooms may not receive as much attention as the other three, their existence shows us a humble yet significant confidence, a beauty that thrives without the need for applause.

Together, these four blossoms offer a vibrant and meaningful metaphor for celebrating our individuality and trusting in our own pace. By studying these blossoms, we can discover a way to live more authentically, while feeling comfortable in our own skin.

Note: Although *ume* (梅) and *sumomo* (李) are both often simply translated as 'plum' in English, *ume* (*Prunus mume*) is in fact botanically more similar to an apricot, while *sumomo* (*Prunus salicina*) is a genuine Japanese plum. Therefore, in this book, 'Japanese apricot blossom' is used for *ume* and 'Japanese plum blossom' for *sumomo*, to reflect their cultural and seasonal differences.

THE WISDOM IN PRACTICE

The wisdom of oubaitori goes beyond the blossoms themselves as it embodies many cultural elements woven into Japanese tradition and rituals. Japanese culture is rich in teachings rooted in mindfulness, nature and the acceptance of impermanence. Customs such as hanami, the art of flower viewing, encourage us to slow down and experience the fleeting beauty of life. Tsukimi, the art of moon viewing, invites us to look up and experience the wonder of the night sky. Practices such as shinrin-yoku, or forest bathing, the practice of mindfully immersing yourself in nature through your senses, remind us of our connection to the earth by demonstrating their healing powers.

The culture of working with our hands also reflects a spirit of mindfulness. An example of this is origami, the traditional Japanese art of paper folding, which embodies presence and the joy of creating something meaningful with simplicity. By exploring our connection with nature and being present in the moment, we can return to our true, whole selves and discover the freedom to express and be at ease with our essence.

Throughout this book, you will discover ways to connect with the wisdom of oubaitori in your daily life, and find ways to reconnect with yourself and the natural world.

HOW THIS BOOK IS STRUCTURED

This book follows the sequence of the oubaitori blossoms, with chapters dedicated to cherry blossoms (*sakura*), Japanese apricot blossoms (*ume*), peach blossoms (*momo*), and Japanese plum blossoms (*sumomo*).

Each chapter offers:

- **Blossom Symbolism:** An exploration of the cultural meanings and significance of each flower.
- **Japanese Wisdom & Practices:** Insights into cultural rituals, traditions, proverbs and creative exercises that bring the teachings to life.
- **Reflections & Insights:** Personal stories and reflections designed to invite understanding and connection.
- **Practical Tips & Reflection Exercises:** Meditations, guided exercises, recipes, simple rituals and tools to integrate the teachings.

The Cherry Blossom chapter invites us to explore impermanence and mindful presence. In the Japanese Apricot Blossom chapter, we will explore the power of resilience. The Peach Blossom chapter invites us to lean into our playful joy and energy. Finally, the Japanese Plum Blossom chapter explores the beauty in inner confidence and humility. These chapters form an explorative journey inwards towards self-discovery, rooted in the rhythms of nature.

AN INVITATION TO BEGIN

As you turn this page, I invite you to embrace yourself as you would a blossom, unique in timing, colour and fragrance. Whether you are just beginning to bloom or have blossomed many times before, remember that your journey is yours alone, worthy of honour, celebration and care.

My hope is that, by the end of this book, the wisdom of oubaitori will inspire you to bloom authentically. You will feel ready to honour your own unique journey and have the tools to return to your true self, celebrating who you are and the life season you are in with patience and self-compassion. I also hope that you will learn to celebrate our differences, allowing us to lead with empathy and come together as a collective whole.

Let us go on your own unique blossoming journey together.

CHAPTER 1

SAKURA

桜

CHERRY BLOSSOMS

The Beauty of Letting Go
and New Beginnings

SAKURA 桜
Cherry Blossoms

Perhaps it comes as no surprise that cherry blossom is the first blossom in the concept of oubaitori. Sakura may be the most famous blossom among the four and is celebrated not only in Japan but across the world.

For many, including myself, cherry blossoms are more than just flowers. They are symbols, feelings and philosophies that invite us to embrace impermanence and give us courage for new beginnings, reminding us of the natural cycle of change.

What makes cherry blossoms so deeply moving is their transient nature. The flowers flourish brilliantly, only to then fall softly soon after, sometimes within days. This fleeting quality, at the core of *hakanasa* (儚さ) and *wabi-sabi* (侘び寂び) – the delicate awareness of life's transience – is at the heart of what this blossom symbolizes. It teaches us that true beauty lies not in permanence or staying the same but in accepting the passage of time. When we can appreciate this ephemeral nature of life, we have the vision to see the preciousness of each moment, giving us the power to be more intentional.

For me, growing up in Japan, cherry blossoms were seamlessly woven into the rhythm of the year and the cycles of life. I remember wondering each year when the cherry blossoms would flourish, eagerly awaiting the weather experts on television to give their yearly predictions. I also remember the years I felt devastated when the cherry blossoms bloomed for only a few short days before a terrible rainy storm. I recall the feeling of awe as I walked home from school, looking up at the sakura namiki – the avenues lined with cherry blossom trees. These moments are all vividly ingrained in my memory and were lessons in mindfulness before I even knew the word, inviting me to be present, to appreciate and to pay attention.

In this chapter, we explore the cherry blossom's deep significance in Japanese culture, from its spiritual connection to its influence on art, poetry and cuisine, and to the communal practice of hanami, where gathering beneath the blossoms becomes both celebration and mindfulness. We'll look at how you can bring this tradition into your own life through food, ritual and community, while also drawing on wisdom principles such as wabi-sabi and hakanasa to embrace imperfection and transience. Alongside cultural insights, you'll find guided meditations and sakura-inspired activities to help you cultivate presence, release what no longer serves you and welcome life's changing seasons with openness.

May this journey exploring the cherry blossoms inspire you to let go of what no longer serves you, to live vibrantly in the present as you appreciate life's fleeting nature and to embrace renewed beginnings.

SYMBOLISM & SIGNIFICANCE OF THE CHERRY BLOSSOM IN JAPAN

While Japan has no official national flower, many would say that the cherry blossom is the one that holds this honour in spirit. Few flowers are as closely tied to Japanese culture, woven through centuries of art, poetry and daily life.

The connection between cherry blossoms and Japanese identity dates back over a thousand years. During the Heian period (794–1185), nobles started having flower-viewing gatherings featuring sakura, which became a symbol of elegance. By the Kamakura period (1192–1333), these gatherings had spread to the samurai class and later, in the Edo period (1603–1868), hanami with cherry blossoms had become a practice embraced by the general public, drawing people from all walks of life to stand beneath the blooms.

This long-standing cultural connection can also be traced through Japan's literary and artistic history. The *Man'yōshū* (万葉集, *Collection of Ten Thousand Leaves*), the oldest collection of Japanese *waka* poetry, compiled in the Nara period (710–794), includes references to cherry blossoms, as does the *Kokin Wakashū* (古今和歌集, *Collection of Ancient and Modern Japanese Poems*) from the Heian period.

Cherry blossoms also appeared frequently in ukiyo-e woodblock prints, which flourished during the Edo period, and in kabuki theatre, where they often provided both backdrop and metaphor. In more recent times, cherry blossoms continue to appear in countless songs, films and seasonal celebrations. Every spring, streets, shops and temples fill with sakura-inspired foods, accessories and decorations, signalling the renewal of the season.

There are many theories as to why cherry blossoms have become so central to Japanese life. Along with them representing a new season, as we come out of a cold, crisp winter, the reason lies in their symbolism of transient, fleeting beauty. Their short-lived bloom reminds us of the impermanence of all things, while also offering the courage of new beginnings. In this way, cherry blossoms embody three deeply Japanese philosophical concepts:

- ***Wabi-sabi*** (侘び寂び): The appreciation of imperfection, impermanence and incompleteness as a natural principle of life. As the cherry blossoms show us, nature is not trying to be perfect, stay the same or be done. This wisdom is a key concept within Japanese culture and is symbolized by the stunning yet short-lived beauty of the cherry blossoms.

- ***Hakanasa*** (儚さ): The gentle awareness of life's transience, impermanence and fragility. The sakura embody this philosophy, which is a key aspect of Japanese culture. As the beautiful petals bloom with such life, they fall to the ground in a short time, reflecting our own human experience of time – brief, fragile and precious. The feelings of sadness in these moments should not be ignored, but held on to and cherished.

- ***Shogyō-Mujō*** (諸行無常)**:** A four-character Japanese Buddhist idiom that signifies how 'all things' (represented by the characters 諸行 *shogyō*) are 'impermanent' (represented by the characters 無常 *mujō*). Referenced in the famous Japanese warrior stories dating back to the 13th and 14th centuries, *The Tale of the Heike* (平家物語 *Heike Monogatari*), this concept reminds us that everything in the world is constantly changing.

These concepts show us why cherry blossoms remain so beloved. They are admired not only for their beauty but also for their wisdom in how to navigate this world. To appreciate them each year is to be reminded of life's fragility, to let go of the need for permanence and to cherish each moment as unique.

HANAKOTOBA – THE FLOWER LANGUAGE OF SAKURA

Japan has a practice known as *hanakotoba* (花言葉), often referred to as the 'language of flowers'. Much like the symbolic meanings given to flowers in other cultures, hanakotoba connects qualities or sentiments to different blossoms. These meanings are not fixed; they have shifted over time, reflecting changing values, poetry and lived experience. Yet they continue to carry an emotional and cultural depth that still resonate with many people in Japan today.

For cherry blossoms, two significant hanakotoba are *seishin-no-bi* (精神の美), which translates to 'spiritual beauty', and *junketsu* (純潔), meaning 'purity'. These meanings mirror what cherry blossoms embody, reminding us that beauty is not measured by how long it lasts, but by the way it blooms vibrantly in the face of the fleeting nature of life. They also remind us that to be truly beautiful, we must not only look beautiful. 'Beauty' in this sense is defined by the internal and spiritual beauty that one has that will shine through. Throughout this book, we will reflect on the hanakotoba of each blossom, as they offer another opportunity to pause and consider our own way of blooming.

WHEN DO CHERRY BLOSSOMS BLOOM?

In Japan, the arrival of cherry blossoms is highly anticipated each year. The timing of their bloom is known as *sakura zensen* (桜前線) – the 'cherry blossom front' – which describes the gradual wave of flowers advancing across the country. The Japan Meteorological Agency records the opening and full bloom of cherry trees each year, allowing people to follow this journey from the southern island of Kyushu all the way up to Hokkaido in the north.

Traditionally, the sakura zensen has moved in a somewhat predictable south-to-north pattern. However, in recent years, the effects of climate change have impacted this rhythm, with blossoms sometimes progressing along unexpected curves. If you are considering visiting Japan for cherry blossom season, it is best to check forecasts early in the year, though it is worth remembering that the exact timing is never guaranteed. While I can understand how some may find this unpredictability frustrating – especially when travel plans are disrupted or sudden changes in weather cause the blossoms to vanish sooner than expected – for me, it is part of their beauty. The uncertainty itself reminds us once more of the impermanence they symbolize.

WHAT DO CHERRY BLOSSOMS LOOK LIKE?

Japan is home to over a hundred varieties of cherry blossoms, both wild and cultivated. Generally, they are characterized by their petals, which split into two at the tip, creating a heart-shaped form. The flower buds grow in clusters, and with their notably long leaf stalks, the blossoms appear to spill from the branches when they bloom.

Among the many, a few stand out as particularly beloved and are widely recognized, offering us a glance into the diversity of sakura across the country.

- ***Somei-yoshino*** **(染井吉野, also called 'Yoshino cherry'):** Known for its delicate clusters of five-petalled flowers, this cultivar is widely planted across Japan. The blossoms begin as pale pink and gradually turn white. Their leaves emerge only after the petals fall, allowing the bloom itself to take centre stage.

- ***Yamazakura*** **(山桜 mountain cherry):** The most common wild species is often found in Japan's mountainous regions – as its name suggests (*yama* means mountain). Its pale pink blossoms open alongside fresh green leaves, creating a striking contrast.

- ***Shidarezakura*** **(枝垂れ桜 weeping cherry tree):** Recognized by their drooping branches, these trees hold a graceful yet dramatic presence. Some shidarezakura are said to be over a thousand years old, standing as living reminders of beauty across centuries.

Each variety of cherry blossom has its own presence, yet together they remind us of the richness of Japan's natural landscape. Let the journey of sakura across the country be more than just a sign of spring – it serves as a reminder of how deeply nature shapes the rhythm of daily life.

DID YOU KNOW?

While most cherry blossoms are shades of pink or white, there is a rare variety called Ukon that blooms with pale, creamy yellow petals.

CHERRY BLOSSOM SPOTS IN JAPAN

Cherry blossoms can be seen all across Japan, with each region offering its own way of observing their ephemeral beauty. While there are numerous places to enjoy them, here are a few sites that give a glimpse into how deeply sakura are woven into the land and spirit of Japan.

A Selection of Cherry Blossom Sites

TAKADA CASTLE SITE PARK (高田城址公園), JŌETSU, NIIGATA (LATE-MARCH TO MID-APRIL*)

With more than 4,000 cherry trees and 3,000 lanterns, Takada Castle Site Park is renowned for having one of the most beautiful evening illuminations in Japan. Walking along the Sakura Road, you pass under a tunnel of blossoms that seem to glow softly in the lantern light when the trees are in full bloom. Experiencing the blossoms here at night offers something unique – a quieter, more contemplative beauty, where the stillness of evening deepens the sense of serenity.

REFLECTION QUESTION: Experiencing the cherry blossoms at night reminds us that beauty is not only found in light. In the stillness of the evening, there is space to notice what often goes unseen. Take a moment to reflect: Where in your own life might you find subtle beauty in unexpected places, even in times that feel dim or uncertain?

MOUNT YOSHINO (吉野山), YOSHINO TOWN, NARA (LATE MARCH TO MID-APRIL*)

Mount Yoshino, or Yoshinoyama, has been one of Japan's most celebrated cherry blossom viewing spots for centuries. With trees said to have been planted more than 1,300 years ago, the mountain is now home to around 30,000 cherry trees, which paint its slopes in soft layers of pink and white from more than 200 varieties. In the summer, you may also encounter Shugendō practitioners known as yamabushi – followers of a Japanese spiritual tradition that blends Buddhism, Shinto, Taoism and mountain worship – reflecting the sacred beliefs long tied to this mountain landscape.

HIROSAKI CASTLE (弘前城), HIROSAKI CITY, AOMORI (MID-APRIL TO EARLY MAY*)

Further north, the grounds of Hirosaki Castle burst into bloom with over 2,500 cherry trees, the majority of them Somei-yoshino. Remarkably, this site is home to one of the oldest Somei-yoshino trees, with many of its blossoms appearing for over a hundred years – far longer than the usual lifespan of around sixty years. Contributing to their longevity is the Hirosaki method, a pruning technique adapted from Aomori's apple orchards. Each year, a team of sakuramori – 'cherry blossom guardians' – care for these trees with patience and precision.

This place also holds a personal place in my heart, as my mother's side of the family comes from Aomori. Though it is not among Japan's most populated or well-known prefectures, knowing that these stunning blossoms appear in the same region that shaped part of my family story makes this site especially meaningful. It is also a reminder for all of us that, just as the blossoms return year after year, our roots and the places we come from deserve a special place in our hearts and are not to be forgotten, even as we move through each new season of life.

PHILOSOPHER'S PATH (哲学の道), KYOTO CITY, KYOTO (EARLY APRIL*)

A stone walkway that follows a canal between Ginkakuji (the Silver Pavilion) and the Nanzenji area, the *Tetsugaku no Michi* (哲学の道), or Philosopher's Path, is lined with hundreds of cherry trees. The path takes its name from Nishida Kitarō, one of Japan's most influential modern philosophers, who is said to have walked here in quiet reflection during his commute to Kyoto University, where he founded what came to be known as the Kyoto School of philosophy.

Nishida sought to express a Zen-inspired understanding of reality through Western-style logic, creating a bridge between Eastern and Western traditions. To walk this path during cherry blossom season is not only to enjoy the beauty of nature, but also to step into a place of mindfulness – echoing Nishida's practice of contemplation under the same flowers.

REFLECTION QUESTION: As you imagine walking beneath the blossoms along the Philosopher's Path, how might you release the weight of the past and arrive more fully in this present moment?

NOTE: *The timing of when the trees will bloom will vary every year based on various climate conditions. The timings given here are provided as general timeframes.*

THE THREE GREAT CHERRY TREES OF JAPAN

A few individual trees are so cherished that they are known as the *Nihon Sandai Zakura* (日本三大桜) – the Three Great Cherry Trees of Japan. Each was designated as a national natural monument in 1922, carrying centuries of history within their branches.

1. Miharu Taki-zakura (三春滝桜)**, Miharu Town, Fukushima Prefecture:** A magnificent *benishidare* (weeping red cherry) with branches cascading like a waterfall, estimated to be more than a thousand years old.

2. Yamataka Jindai-zakura (山高神代桜)**, Hokuto City, Yamanashi Prefecture:** An enormous *edohigan* cherry, a wild species believed to be between 1,800 and 2,000 years old. Said to be Japan's oldest and largest cherry tree of this variety, it stands as a living witness to countless generations.

3. Neodani Usuzumi-zakura (根尾谷淡墨桜)**, Motosu City, Gifu Prefecture:** Said to have been planted by Emperor Keitai, the 26th emperor of Japan, this towering tree is at least 1,500 years old. Its blossoms are unique: they open pale pink, turn pure white and finally fade to a soft ink-like grey. Its name reflects this transformation: *usu* (淡) meaning pale, *sumi* (墨) meaning ink, and *sakura* (桜) meaning cherry blossom.

These trees remind us that sakura are not only fleeting moments of beauty, but also enduring presences that have connected people across centuries. To stand before them is to feel both the joy of blossoms and the resilience of nature itself. They also offer perspective: our human lives, with all their worries and concerns, are brief in comparison to nature's span. Some may find this sobering, but I find this grounding – a way to remember that our lies are part of a much larger, more vast time horizon.

A MOMENT OF REFLECTION

As you read about these places and trees, notice where your attention settles. Is it on the thousands of blossoms filling the mountainside in Nara, or perhaps the single weeping cherry blossom tree that has stood for more than a thousand years? Whatever draws you is a soft intuition – allow yourself to honour it.

TAKE A MOMENT TO REFLECT ON YOUR INSTINCT: What am I being invited to release right now, so that something new can take shape? How might I cherish each moment more deeply, knowing it will not last forever?

Just as the cherry blossoms remind us that every petal that falls follows the natural rhythm of life, making way for renewal, your own season of change may be unfolding before you.

RESPECTING THE SAKURA AS AN ACT OF MINDFULNESS

The presence of the cherry blossoms is fleeting and precious. When we gather to enjoy them, our role is to honour them so that others may enjoy their beauty as well. Respecting the blossoms is an act of mindfulness. By treating them with care, we learn to slow down, to notice and to honour the beauty that surrounds us – nurturing a deeper connection with both nature and one another.

- **Do not bend or cut the branches.** Even a small break can cause lasting harm to the tree.
- **Avoid placing objects on the branches or blossoms.** However light they may seem, they can still damage the flowers.
- **Let the petals fall naturally.** Please resist the urge to shake the branches; part of the beauty is in allowing nature to unfold in its own rhythm.
- **Respect boundaries around the trees.** If an area is roped off, it is to protect both the trees and the delicate soil beneath them.
- **Care for the trunks and roots.** Avoid leaning heavily against the trees or disturbing the ground nearby, as this is part of a delicate ecosystem.
- **Admire the trees from below.** Climbing may seem tempting, but these blossoms are best appreciated with both feet on the ground.
- **Be mindful of others around you.** Sakura season is a shared experience, and small acts of kindness ensure everyone can enjoy the view.

JAPAN'S CONNECTION TO NATURE

To understand Japan's deep connection to nature, let's first take a look at its landscape. Japan is a long archipelago comprising four large islands – Hokkaido, Honshu, Shikoku and Kyushu – along with numerous smaller islands. It is a land of plentiful nature – roughly three-quarters of the country is mountainous and forests cover about two-thirds of it. This terrain has influenced not only how people live but also how they see themselves in relation to the natural world. Mountains, rivers, forests and water are considered to be more than scenery; they are essential in shaping a worldview that honours nature as a teacher much greater than humans.

This appreciation is connected to Shinto, one of Japan's primary religions alongside Buddhism. Shinto is Japan's indigenous nature-based spirituality, often translated as 'the way of the spirits'. It is a belief system that shows devotion to the *kami* (spirits), which inhabit all things, embracing the forces of nature including the wind, rain and earth. Shinto does not have a founder or a single god, nor does it require strict adherence. Because of this unique understanding, many in Japan do not view Shinto as a religion in the Western sense, but rather as an integral part of Japanese life and culture. With more than 70,000 Shinto shrines across the country, this connection to the natural world cannot go unnoticed. To bow before a tree, or to feel awe at a mountainous landscape, is not unusual; it is part of recognizing the sacredness of nature and appreciating how humans exist through its grace.

This cultural relationship with nature continues into modern wellbeing practices, most recognizably in recent years through *shinrin-yoku* (森林浴), or 'forest bathing'. First named and studied in Japan by the Forestry Agency in the 1980s, shinrin-yoku emerged as both a response to rising urban stress and a way of reconnecting with the health benefits of time spent in the forest. Research in Japan has shown that walking mindfully through nature, breathing deeply and engaging the senses can reduce cortisol levels, boost immune function and improve mental health. At its heart, though, shinrin-yoku is not about exercise or goals – it is about presence, allowing nature to enter your body, mind and soul.

DID YOU KNOW?

The Japanese 100-yen coin features cherry blossoms. A small but meaningful reminder that Japan's connection to nature is not only found in poetry, art or festivals, but even in the everyday act of shopping.

PRACTISING SHINRIN-YOKU

While you may not always find yourself near mountains or forests, the essence of shinrin-yoku can be carried into everyday life. Whether you are taking a walk in a nearby park, pausing during a hike or simply noticing the trees outside your window, here are a few simple ways to integrate forest bathing into your routine today.

Engage with your senses: Reconnect with your five senses – smell, sight, touch, hearing and taste. What sounds of nature do you hear? Can you feel the ground beneath you as you take each step? What scents rise from the plants and trees around you? What colours capture your attention? For taste, be careful not to eat anything wild without proper guidance. As an alternative, when you next taste vegetables as part of a meal, pause to notice their flavours more closely – this, too, is a way of reconnecting with your senses.

Go device-free: Consider leaving your phone and headphones at home while you walk outside. While convenient, these devices often distract us from connecting with the natural world. Without them, we open the possibility for a stronger presence of nature in our lives.

Enjoy a slow pace: Notice how quickly you are moving. The beauty of forest bathing comes from recognizing that there is no rush. Take your time and let yourself be moved by awe and appreciation, unmeasured by minutes or steps.

Bring nature indoors: Place a plant on your desk, arrange a bouquet of flowers in a vase or fill a bowl with seasonal fruits or vegetables. Small gestures like these reconnect you to the rhythms of nature.

Add a mindfulness ritual outdoors: Sip tea beneath a tree, read in the park or journal by the water. Choose rituals that feel natural to you, and let them root you in your surroundings.

Invite a friend: Suggest a walk in the park instead of sitting in a café, or take a coworker outside for a coffee break. Blending community and nature can uplift and recharge your spirit.

Japan's relationship with nature is a living wisdom that reminds us how profoundly our wellbeing is tied to the world around us. Though many of these ideas have Japanese origins, they resonate with a universal message: nature is a sacred gift that sustains us, that we are called to cherish, care for and honour. Perhaps this is the reminder we all need – that our collective home is Mother Earth, and we owe it to the land, to ourselves and to one another to connect with it every day.

HANAMI: THE ART OF FLOWER VIEWING

Personal Memories of Hanami

When I reflect on my hanami memories, I feel my shoulders soften, my breath deepen and a natural smile emerging. Growing up in Tokyo, long avenues of cherry blossom trees lined the streets near my local subway station. My family and I would take walks on the weekends and watch with wonder as the buds slowly formed, eventually blossomed and finally fell from their branches with the passing of the spring days.

What was fascinating about these moments was that they never felt like we were enjoying the blossoms alone. Locals often gathered to appreciate the sakura namiki (cherry blossom avenues). In those shared moments, they didn't feel like strangers. Even if we didn't exchange words, we shared a mutual gratitude for the cherry blossoms. I still carry the warm energy of those memories, an internal feeling of connection.

The timing of when the cherry trees bloom varies slightly across Japan, as it is influenced by the local climate. Every year, we would attentively follow news reports predicting the arrival of the blossoms. Those forecasts carried a sense of renewal and eagerness as we waited for the cherry blossoms to arrive.

While I am currently thousands of miles from Japan, these memories continue to ground me. They connect me to my culture, to family, to the rhythm of nature and to the collective experience of being fully present in a shared moment.

A SENSORY CELEBRATION

To truly understand hanami is to awaken all the senses. It is not merely about looking at flowers but about *being* with them in a full-bodied, mindful way.

Imagine standing under a medley of pale pink and white blossoms. The blossoms form an arch above you, with sunlight filtering through the branches. You can feel a gentle breeze from behind you, causing the petals to drift slowly from the branches to the ground, as if they are dancing slowly and willingly to their fate. The air is full of the sweet fragrance of the blossoms and the earthy aroma of the soil.

Around you, laughter and comfortable silence fill the air as friends share stories and enjoy their time together. Delicious seasonal dishes such as sakura mochi, a wagashi rice cake wrapped in a fragrant cherry blossom leaf, or traditional onigiri rice balls satisfy your appetite.

In these moments, time feels spacious, asking you to slow down and take your time. Hanami invites us to savour the present; as the word itself suggests, it is the gift that we often forget to give ourselves.

HANAMI BEYOND THE CHERRY BLOSSOMS

While hanami is most commonly associated with cherry blossoms, the broader Japanese concept of oubaitori reminds us that other blossoms also have their time and beauty. Japanese apricot (*ume*), peach (*momo*) and Japanese plum (*sumomo*) each bloom at their own time and in their own way, none claiming to outshine the others.

This insight invites us to appreciate the beauty in our individuality and timing. To celebrate this, hanami should be embraced throughout the year, honouring not only the other oubaitori blossoms, but the vast beauty that nature has to offer.

CREATE YOUR OWN HANAMI EXPERIENCE

PREPARING FOR YOUR HANAMI

Hanami is not merely a picnic, it is a mindful, purposeful way to connect with and appreciate nature's beauty as well as an invitation to connect with the cycles of your own internal life. Intentional preparation is a meaningful way to slow down and gives us the space to arrive holistically and authentically.

LOCATION

The first step in preparing for your hanami is deciding on the location. If you are lucky enough to have cherry blossoms nearby, whether in a local park or a garden, you can plan your gathering around their flowering season. If you do not have cherry blossoms locally, there is no need to worry. The art of hanami can be appreciated with any bloom, as it is the intention behind it that makes the practice truly meaningful.

Find your own unique place where spring unfolds – a local park, a nature reserve, a community garden, or perhaps even your balcony with a view. Maybe the blossoms are bluebells, snowdrops or even primroses; the list of seasonal flowers is vast and abundant. What matters most is your presence and your openness to the natural world around you.

PEOPLE

As you prepare your gathering, consider who you would like to share this time with. It is important to invite people whose energy lifts your spirits and nourishes your heart. Powerful questions to reflect on are: *How do I feel after spending time with this person? Do they charge my personal batteries or drain them?* Allow yourself to listen honestly to your answers. Hanami is a space for warmth, presence and renewal. Surround yourself with those who help you feel this, whether it's family members, friends or colleagues – or it could be a solo gathering.

COMFORT

Once you have found your hanami location and the individuals you would like to share this experience with, create a welcoming space that feels open and genuine. You can bring a picnic and a soft blanket to sit on, or perhaps you prefer to carry some portable chairs. What is important is that you are creating a space where you feel comfortable. This will and should look different for each of us.

INTENTION

As you prepare for your hanami experience, remember that it is as much about your intention as it is about nature's beauty. Before you head out, pause and set your *kokoro-zashi* (志), the Japanese word for intention, which translates as 'heartfelt intention'. The Japanese kanji (character) for *kokoro-zashi* (志) carries a beautiful meaning – '*going in the direction your heart is longing to go*'. This is a hint for us to listen to our heart and soul, rather than be led by our mind.

Your kokoro-zashi may be a simple desire to find ease, to celebrate renewal, to cultivate gratitude or to connect with loved ones or yourself. Whatever it may be, let's welcome it wholeheartedly. Let it be a guiding light for you during your hanami experience, amplifying your experience with intention.

SETTING YOUR KOKORO-ZASHI

Take a moment to close your eyes, take a few deep breaths, and put your hand on your heart. Feel your heartbeat and acknowledge the intention you will be bringing to your hanami experience. This intentional beginning invites you to slow down, to feel fully and to honour this time you have created for yourself.

COOK YOUR HANAMI

One of the joyous parts of hanami is sharing food – a delicious and meaningful way to connect with the season, with others and with yourself. Enjoying a meal with people is a universal ritual across the world that brings people together. Colours, textures and aromas come to life in traditional hanami cuisine, which is a sensory feast as well as a celebration of nature's gifts.

A hanami picnic typically features a bento box filled with a variety of small dishes, thoughtfully chosen to reflect seasonal delicacies and celebrate spring. The foods should be bite-sized or easy to divide, as they should be perfect for sharing and being mindfully eaten while enjoying the flowers.

If you would like to bring a few traditional hanami treats to your experience, here are a few options. You could try *sakura mochi* (桜餅), a delicate pink rice cake cooked with a red bean paste wrapped in a salted cherry blossom leaf, along with *kusamochi* (草餅), mochi infused with yomogi, or Japanese mugwort. Both treats are Japanese wagashi, or confectionery, and will infuse nature's seasonal gifts into the eating experience. Another classic hanami treat is *hanami dango* (花見団子), often called *sanshoku dango* (三色団子) – a skewer of three different-coloured rice dumplings, each colour symbolizing different elements of nature. There are various theories about the origins of these colours, and one suggests that they represent the rhythms of nature. Pink symbolizes cherry blossoms, indicating the arrival of spring; white represents snow, reflecting the excitement of winter coming to an end; while green signifies the new leaves that emerge after spring has begun. These simple nibbles capture the spirit of the season in both flavour and symbolism.

On the savoury side, traditional rice dishes such as *onigiri* (rice balls), *inarizushi* (rice wrapped in tofu pockets), or *makizushi* (rolled sushi) are all accessible options. Luckily, you can typically find these dishes at your local Asian supermarket if you would like to bring a little taste of the Japanese experience with you.

While I have shared a few traditional hanami food options, the beauty is that you can make and bring whatever you want. The primary focus is to use seasonal produce and, if you decide to have your hanami experience with others, to make the dishes relatively easy to share.

If you enjoy cooking, this can be an opportunity to prepare these foods with mindful attention and gratitude. Take the time to notice the texture of the rice grains as you wash them, the varying colours of the finished dishes and the inviting aromas.

Food in hanami is more than just nourishment, it is a tried and tested way to connect. Sharing these seasonal dishes with others reflects the collective spirit of hanami, an intentional coming together to honour nature's fleeting beauty with those who matter. Even if you gather alone, preparing and eating these foods with mindfulness can deepen your connection to life cycles.

If you would like to try a simple dish, overleaf is an onigiri recipe that can easily be customized to your preference for your hanami gathering.

Classic Onigiri (Rice Balls)

Makes six

Onigiri are Japanese rice balls wrapped in nori (sheets of dried seaweed). Classic fillings include grilled salmon flakes, pickled ume (*umeboshi*), simmered kombu (*tsukudani*) or bonito flakes mixed with soy sauce (*okaka*). If you prefer to keep things simple, just seasoning the rice with sea salt flakes is a great traditional option. All these ingredients can usually be found at Japanese or Asian supermarkets, though mainstream supermarkets are increasingly stocking them too.

600g (3 cups) freshly cooked Japanese short-grain rice (about 200g/1 cup uncooked rice)
Sushi nori seaweed
Fillings of your choice

1. Allow the cooked rice to cool until just warm enough to handle safely.
2. Put a small handful of rice (about 100g/½ cup) into a small bowl.
3. If you're opting for no fillings, sprinkle sea salt evenly over the rice to your desired seasoning level. Alternatively, place a small amount of your chosen filling in the centre of the rice.
4. To prevent the rice sticking, wet your hands. Gently but firmly press the rice around the filling, shaping it into a compact ball or pyramid.
5. Wrap the rice ball in a strip of nori seaweed – this adds a depth of flavour and a contrast in texture.
6. Repeat the process with the remaining rice, varying the fillings for colour and taste if you wish.
7. Place the rice balls in a bento box or wrap each one individually with plastic wrap to keep them fresh.

MINDFULNESS TIP: As you prepare these rice balls, slow down and focus on each movement and step. Feel the softness of the rice, smell the toasty aroma of the seaweed and notice the different textures of your fillings. Bring to mind your hanami intention and let the mindful preparation bring you calm and ease.

DURING YOUR HANAMI

When you arrive at your hanami spot, take a few deep breaths. Make the time to feel grounded. Allow yourself to slow down and fully arrive; this is your time to be present.

TECHNOLOGY

Consider a device audit, where you check the technology you have with you. Can you switch your phone to silent mode or put your devices away? This is an act of self-care, inviting you to remove distractions that can pull you away from connecting with nature and those who have gathered with you.

SENSES

As you sit underneath the blossoms, lean into your senses. What colours do you see filling up the canvas in front of you? Can you see the petals delicately drifting from their branches? Which sounds of nature make up the background? Perhaps this is the sound of birdsong or the soft rustle of leaves. How would you describe the aromas of the blossoms and nature that surround you? Do not rush or put a time limit on this experience. You are here to simply be.

GRATITUDE

Before you begin to eat, consider practising the Japanese tradition of *itadakimasu* (いただきます). We say this phrase out loud in Japan before a meal with our hands facing each other, and it means '*I humbly receive*'. It is a gratitude phrase where we give thanks for the nourishing food in front of us, the hands that prepared it, the farmers who cultivated it and the life that sustains us. Let this phrase offer a moment to appreciate and respect your gathering.

COMMUNITY

Hanami is as much about community as it is about nature. If you are sharing your experience with others, allow the conversations to flow naturally. You may share thoughts on the changing seasons, favourite memories outdoors or simple gratitude for the moment. At the same time, welcome the silence. It can be such a gift to enjoy the comfort and beauty of nature alongside one another and connect that sometimes words fall short.

PHOTO

You may consider taking photos to document your experience or choose to put your camera away entirely. If you decide to capture some moments, do so mindfully, taking your time with each photo and appreciating the view you are capturing.

BREATH

If you find your mind getting distracted or your thoughts wandering, pay attention to your breath. Let it be an anchor to bring you back to your body, taking you back to presence through the power of your five senses. This simple, powerful practice can empower your hanami experience even more.

CLEAN-UP

As your hanami comes to a close, let's take care of the space that welcomed you by thoughtfully cleaning up after yourself. This shows respect to Mother Nature, who has given us this precious experience, and ensures others can share its beauty.

Let the presence of your community, the delicate beauty of the blooms and the feelings you feel within sink in. Know that you can carry this experience with you long after the petals have fallen.

AFTER YOUR HANAMI

As you wrap up your hanami experience, take a moment to reflect.

Whenever you feel drawn to pause and look back at your experience, invite yourself to sit in stillness and be present with yourself. This can be done immediately after your hanami or a few days later – no urgency or rigid structure needed is needed. Just allow the thoughts, feelings or memories to surface naturally.

Reflection is not about finding the 'right' answers; it is the practice of opening a space where your experience can settle internally.

A few helpful questions that you could reflect on:

- What feelings surfaced as you appreciated nature's beauty?
- How did your body feel during your hanami experience?
- Did anything surprise or touch you unexpectedly?
- What memories or moments have stayed with you?
- Did reflections on new beginnings or letting go come to the surface?
- Which parts of the hanami experience were most joyful?

Sharing your hanami experience can also be a gift. Whether through photos, creative writing or simple conversations, opening space for others to learn about your story can inspire connection and invite them into this practice.

It is powerful to know you can carry these reflections and your hanami intention forwards into daily life. Perhaps it is a reminder to pause and take a deep breath to connect with your body before a busy day, to cook seasonal dishes mindfully, to notice nature blooming or petals falling during your commute, or to enjoy the company of others without any distractions. Bring the rituals you enjoyed during hanami into your everyday life to support your continued connection.

Remember that hanami is an experience that you can create throughout the seasons and is a practice that is always available to you. May the joy and calm you cultivated under the blossoms continue to gently bloom within you, carrying you into each new beginning.

PRACTICE: SAKURA VISUALIZATION – LETTING GO AND EMBRACING THE NEW

This guided visualization invites you to gently release what no longer serves you and open your heart to fresh beginnings, inspired by the symbolic, stunning and transient beauty of cherry blossoms.

THE VISUALIZATION

Find a quiet space. Sit or lie down comfortably. Close your eyes gently and begin by bringing your attention to your breath. Inhale slowly through your nose, filling your lungs with peaceful ease. Exhale slowly through your mouth, releasing any tension with kindness. Continue for a couple more breaths, allowing yourself to arrive fully in this moment.

Now, imagine you are standing under a canopy of cherry blossoms in full bloom. Above you, the petals are present in abundance; they are delicate pale pink and white, glowing with a sense of lightness and warmth, inviting you to pause and simply be. The delicate petals flutter in the breeze, making soft waves of motion. Feel the warmth of the sun on your skin, and the fresh, sweet scent of blossoms filling the air.

As you watch the petals dance and slowly fall around you, notice how naturally they let go of their attachment to the branches, surrendering to nature's energy without resistance.

With each breath, imagine yourself releasing a thought, a worry, a weight you have been carrying. Just as a petal effortlessly drifts down and is carried by the wind, feel this release float away. Allow yourself to soften into this moment of letting go.

The moment holds you. It supports you and welcomes you into this new beginning.

Know that just as the petals fall to make way for new growth, you too can release what no longer serves your wellbeing, your authentic self, your journey.

Feel the space that opens within you as you let go. The sense of lightness in your chest; the room for renewal, for possibility, for expansion.

Breathe in deeply and welcome this fresh energy. Breathe out fully and feel yourself grounded in calm acceptance.

Take a moment here beneath the cherry blossoms, wrapped in their serene presence, knowing you are part of this continuous cycle of blooming and releasing.

Take a few more breaths. Wiggle your fingers and toes softly, feeling your body alive and present. When you feel ready, slowly open your eyes, carrying the grace of the sakura, the courage to let go and the openness to embrace new beginnings with you into the rest of your day.

CHAPTER WRAP-UP

As our chapter on cherry blossoms comes to a close, take a moment to notice what has shifted within you. Perhaps it is a slower pace of breath, a moment of wonder at nature's beauty or a realization that it is time to let go of something in your life that no longer serves you. Whatever it may be, it is a reminder that your life will continue to unfold in seasons, and you are not only allowed, but expected, to start again, to evolve, to continue moving forwards.

The sakura teaches us to meet each moment fully and then release it with grace. By learning to let go and appreciate impermanence, we create space for the new to arrive. And if a worry returns, you can come back to these practices and rituals – anchoring yourself in groundedness and patience as renewal enters in small, progressive ways.

In the next chapter, we turn to the Japanese apricot (*ume*), the blossom that dares to open while winter still lingers. Where sakura teaches the grace of letting go, ume offers the courage to endure and the strength to bloom through difficulty.

CHAPTER 2

UME
梅

JAPANESE APRICOT BLOSSOMS

Blooming through Challenges and Fostering Resilience

UME 梅
Japanese Apricot Blossoms

When winter still lingers, and the air carries its crispness, Japanese apricot blossoms begin to bloom. In Japan, there is a saying, *ume wa hyakka no sakigake* (梅は百花の魁), meaning 'the Japanese apricot blossom is the forerunner of a hundred flowers'. It is also used to describe individuals who step forwards before others, leading not by force but through courage and perseverance. From late January through April, their flowers appear before almost every other bloom, standing as a gentle yet convincing reminder that life does not wait for flawless conditions.

While the cherry blossom has become the most widely recognized symbol of Japan in recent years, the Japanese apricot blossom holds a much older and more deeply rooted place in Japanese culture. In the *Man'yōshū* (万葉集), the oldest surviving collection of Japanese poetry compiled in the Nara period (710–794), Japanese apricot blossoms are mentioned more often than almost any other flower except the Japanese bush clover (*hagi* 萩). Their abundant presence in these verses speaks to the admiration and intimacy the Japanese people have long felt towards them.

The beauty of ume lies in its variety. With over 300 cultivars, these blossoms can be soft white, pale pink or deep crimson. Some change colour as they open, as if carrying within them the story of transformation, while others carry a delicate blush or red at the edges, as if the winter's chill touches them. Each variety of Japanese apricot blossom, whether modest or striking, connects us with the power of resilience – the ability to bloom in different forms, even when the environment is challenging.

Japanese apricot blossom also carries strong cultural and spiritual connections. A well-known story in Japan is that of Sugawara no Michizane, a prominent scholar and poet during the Heian period (794–1185) who was later deified as Tenjin, the god of learning in Shinto. It is said that he loved these blossoms deeply. Even today, shrines dedicated to Tenjin honour this bloom by incorporating it into their *shinmon* (神紋) or shrine crests, and by planting many Japanese apricot trees within their grounds. These symbols remind us of the enduring link between ume flowers and resilience, perseverance and courage.

For me, ume also carries a personal memory. When I was a child, my grandmother would offer me a rice ball with umeboshi – a salted, pickled ume – tucked into the centre. On hot summer days, she would tell me that it would help me feel better. At first, the taste was startling: sour, salty, almost overwhelming – and I did not enjoy it. Yet, over time, I grew to appreciate the taste, finding comfort in its sharpness. I can see now how this memory connects me to resilience. At the beginning, discomfort can almost feel unbearable, but with time and patience what once seemed challenging can evolve into a source of strength. I sense the same lesson in the Japanese apricot blossom: resilience is not about avoiding hardship, but learning to transform through it.

In this chapter, we will dive into the cultural and symbolic depth of the Japanese apricot blossom: its role in poetry and Japanese culture, as well as its place in Japanese cuisine. We will reflect on sayings and stories that connect us to resilience and perseverance. You will also find simple practices – such as tea rituals, daily resilience practices and creative writing – that can help you foster resilience in your own life.

May the lessons of the Japanese apricot blossom encourage you to honour your inner strength, to endure with grace and to trust that even in seasons of difficulty, you too can bloom.

SYMBOLISM & SIGNIFICANCE OF THE JAPANESE APRICOT BLOSSOM IN JAPAN

The Japanese apricot blossom is one of Japan's most representative trees, admired not only for its beauty but also for its practical use in food and medicine. Before cherry blossoms rose to prominence, the Japanese apricot blossom held centre stage in seasonal flower-viewing traditions.

This appreciation is said to have begun in the Nara period (710–794), when noblemen, influenced by cultural exchange with China, gathered beneath the fragrant Japanese apricot trees to compose poetry. Many of these early traditional Japanese poems followed the structure of the *tanka* (短歌), meaning 'short song', with five lines and a total of 31 syllables (5–7–5–7–7). These gatherings marked the beginnings of the hanami traditions that Japan continues to cherish today.

Japanese apricot blossoms appear in over 100 poems in the *Man'yōshū*, far more than cherry blossoms, reflecting the admiration the Japanese people held for Japanese apricot from the earliest times. The blossoms came to symbolize purity and an indomitable spirit; they were admired for their ability to endure the cold and bloom at the threshold of spring. This symbolism extended into samurai culture and literature, where the ume was seen as a reminder of strength, courage and perseverance.

Beyond symbolism, the Japanese apricot blossom also played a role in Japan's medical and culinary history. Japan's oldest surviving medical text, the *Ishinpō* (984), mentions umeboshi (pickled ume) for their health and sterilizing properties. A well-known story tells of Emperor Murakami, who, during the Heian period (794–1185), recovered from illness after drinking tea infused with umeboshi and kombu seaweed. This tea, called ōbukucha, is still enjoyed today as an auspicious drink around the New Year. During the

Kamakura period (1192–1333), pickled Japanese apricot spread further, and it was said that samurai carried them into battle, both for their energizing properties and their association with good fortune.

The cultural significance of Japanese apricot is also reflected in the present day. Japan's current imperial era, *Reiwa* (令和), which began on 1 May 2019, draws its name from a passage found in classical Japanese poetry that celebrates the Japanese apricot blossoms that arrive in early spring.

The Japanese prime minister at the time explained that the era name embodied hope for Japan to be a nation where, like the Japanese apricot blossoms blooming after a challenging winter, each individual could flourish fully while carrying forwards their hopes for tomorrow. The system of imperial era names continues to hold profound cultural significance in Japan, appearing not only in official documents but also in unity with the hearts and souls of the population.

From traditional poetry to modern times, the ume remains a flower of resilience and hope – teaching us that strength is not the absence of hardship but the courage to bloom even in the cold.

HANAKOTOBA – THE FLOWER LANGUAGE OF UME

For Japanese apricot blossoms, three powerful words are 忍耐 (*nintai*), which translates to 'perseverance', 忠実 (*chūjitsu*), meaning 'loyalty' and 高潔 (*kōketsu*), meaning 'acting with noble character and integrity'.

These meanings invite us to pause and reflect. The Japanese apricot blossoms teach us that, by living with integrity and staying loyal to our virtues, we can build a life of resilience. How might we foster such qualities in our own lives today? Aligning with our values through small, everyday actions can be a powerful way to incorporate the lesson of the Japanese apricot blossoms.

PRACTICE: RESILIENCE DAILY TIPS

Resilience is a word we often hear, but how can we practise it in everyday life? At its heart, it is the ability to adapt to life's challenges with a sense of flexibility. In wellness, we understand that it touches various dimensions of our lives – from our emotional, spiritual and environmental elements to our social, physical, financial, occupational and intellectual sides.

When we reflect on this, it shows us that resilience is a living process rather than a trait we either possess or lack. It also emphasizes the many dimensions in which we can practise this skill, enabling us to adapt to life experiences with greater flexibility in response to both external demands and internal challenges.

It can be challenging to know which avenue in our lives to start building this resilience muscle. Here are a few Japanese sayings and concepts that speak to the different dimensions of life that may help in weaving resilience into your everyday life:

Find your *nakama* (仲間): Resilience grows when we don't face challenges alone. Nakama is a Japanese word for a companion or friend with whom you share a deep connection, and speaks to the social dimension of life. When thinking of who would be in your nakama, check in on how you feel after spending time with a person – if they elevate your spirits and energy, this is a positive sign. Consider who your nakama might be, and how you can nurture this relationship to support each other in times of need.

Take time to find your *ikigai* (生き甲斐): Having a sense of purpose can help us to navigate difficult times by serving as a guiding light. While often mistranslated as a Venn diagram, ikigai roughly translates to 'reason for being' and refers to the moments or avenues in your life that give your life purpose. Part of your spiritual wellbeing, this can be rooted in your professional or personal life, despite common misinterpretations that it is exclusively tied to your job. To start building a sense of ikigai, take time to reflect: What moments in your day get you up in the morning and give you direction?

Adopt the perspective of *shōganai* (しょうがない): This Japanese phrase reflects the acceptance that some things are beyond our control. Applicable to all dimensions of life, recognizing the distinction between what we can and cannot change widens our perspective and releases unnecessary struggle. Try a simple audit: What is within your control, and what is not? How can you cultivate an acceptance mindset to gain clarity and a sense of agency?

Focus on small, steady actions with *amadare ishi o ugatsu* (雨垂れ石を穿つ): This proverb, which translates to 'the constant dripping of water wears away a stone', reminds us that true resilience is built not through grand gestures, but through small, consistent efforts. Even the finest, seemingly insignificant raindrops, by persistently falling on the same spot, can eventually create a hole in a hard stone. This illustrates the power of consistent, small actions. Ask yourself: What small daily action, taken patiently, could gradually transform my life?

Build self-belief with *futō fukutsu* (不撓不屈)**:** This four-character idiom combines *futō* (unyielding) and *fukutsu* (invincible) to describe an unbreakable spirit – one that does not give in, no matter the difficulty. It is a popular Japanese phrase that many people live by. While it may be challenging to embody this concept fully from the beginning, its essence lies in nurturing belief in yourself. Do you believe in your own ability to be resilient? This belief alone is a vital part of resilience. Let this phrase inspire you to believe that resilience grows when you trust in your ability to endure.

Just as the Japanese apricot blossoms bloom against the cold of late winter, resilience is about finding strength even when conditions feel less than ideal. Many of us can relate to this when our environment or circumstances seem to work against us. By drawing on concepts that nurture our resilience, we plant seeds of strength that can grow over time.

WHEN DO JAPANESE APRICOT BLOSSOMS BLOOM?

When winter still lingers, the first sign of spring's arrival in Japan often comes with the Japanese Apricot blossoms. Known as *sōshun no hana* (早春の花), or the 'earliest flowers of spring', some Japanese Apricot varieties begin to bloom as early as late December, their petals opening against the crisp, cold air. For most, the season spans from late January to April, making them a symbol of the transition into spring. Japanese Apricot blossoms sweep northwards across the archipelago, though their timing depends on climate, region and variety. In Kyushu, blooms often begin in late January. In the Kansai region, they appear from early February, while in Kanto, including Tokyo, they arrive around mid-February. By the time spring reaches the colder northern prefectures of Tohoku, it is early March, and finally in Hokkaido, the blossoms do not open until late April.

These are only general guidelines, for ume are known for their diversity – more than 300 varieties exist, each with its own rhythm. Some open when winter is still sharp, while others wait for softer conditions. This unpredictability, I feel, is part of their whispered teaching: resilience does not follow one fixed timetable. Just as each blossom opens in its own moment, our own perseverance should follow its own timing.

WHAT DO JAPANESE APRICOT BLOSSOMS LOOK LIKE?

Japanese Apricot blossoms are distinct in both their form and character. Known for their strong and pleasant fragrance, they carry an unmistakable presence, often noticed before they are seen. Their petals are rounded, and each flower grows directly from the branch, clinging close without leaf stalks. Unlike trees with heavy clusters of flowers, Japanese Apricots have one bud per node, creating a more sparse but dignified appearance. The leaves emerge only after the flowers have bloomed, allowing the blossoms to hold the stage.

Horticulturally, Japanese Apricot trees are often divided into two groups. *Hana-ume* (花梅) are cultivated for flower-viewing and celebrated for their seasonal beauty, while *mi-ume* (実梅) are grown primarily for their fruit, used in Japanese cuisine such as umeboshi (pickled ume) and umeshu (ume wine). Among the hana-ume, three broad categories capture the variety of the Japanese apricot:

- ***Yabai-kei*** (野梅系): Thought to be closest to the original wild ume introduced from China, these trees have comparatively small leaves and flowers but carry a strong, captivating fragrance. Within this group lie numerous variations, each modest yet striking in its own way.

- ***Hibai-kei*** (緋梅系): Said to have evolved from the yabai-kei, these trees are known for their reddish bark and crimson or scarlet flowers. Their vibrant blossoms often stand out in gardens, and they are also popular for bonsai cultivation.

- ***Bungo-kei*** (豊後系): A hybrid between plum and apricot, these trees thrive and have larger leaves and often pink-coloured flowers. Their blossoms carry both the strength of Japanese apricot and the softness of Japanese plum, displaying beauty in their unique form.

These variations remind us that even within Japanese Apricot blossoms, diversity flourishes. Through their vibrant appearance and fragrance, they show us that resilience is found in trusting our own unique timing.

DID YOU KNOW?

One easy way to tell Japanese apricot blossoms apart from cherry blossoms is by looking at their petals. Japanese apricot petals are rounded and smooth at the tip, while cherry petals feature a small notch that creates a gentle split, giving them a heart-shaped appearance.

JAPANESE APRICOT BLOSSOM SITES

To experience Japanese apricot blossoms in their fullest bloom, a great place to start is in the Kanto region, at one of the three sites collectively known as the **Kantō Sandai Bairin** (関東三大梅林) – the Three Great Ume Groves of Kanto.

THE THREE GREAT UME GROVES OF KANTO

Each of the three sites carries its own history, character and atmosphere, yet all celebrate the same message of resilience and renewal.

KAIRAKUEN GARDEN (偕楽園), MITO CITY, IBARAKI PREFECTURE (MID-FEBRUARY TO MARCH*)

One of Japan's Three Great Gardens, Kairakuen Garden is home to around 3,000 Japanese apricot trees, representing nearly 100 varieties. These include the celebrated 'Six Famous Trees of Mito', varieties distinguished by their unique form and scent. Each year from mid-February to mid-March, the Mito Ume Festival brings the garden to life, offering visitors a chance to appreciate the blossoms while honouring years of tradition.

SOGA UME GROVE (曽我梅林), ODAWARA CITY, KANAGAWA PREFECTURE (EARLY FEBRUARY TO EARLY MARCH*)

The Soga Ume Grove dates back more than 600 years, to when many Japanese apricot trees were planted in Odawara to provide provisions for soldiers. These trees were then used during the Edo period to make umeboshi for travellers crossing the Hakone mountains. Today, more than 35,000 white ume trees bloom here, creating a vast and fragrant landscape. The city honours them with an annual festival, which attracts visitors from across Japan, especially because of the stunning view of Mount Fuji that accompanies the blossoms.

OGOSE UME GROVE (越生梅林), OGOSE TOWN, SAITAMA PREFECTURE (MID-FEBRUARY TO MID-MARCH*)

Ogose boasts more than 20,000 Japanese apricot trees. In early spring, the air is filled with the aroma of the trees. Among the grove's gems is the Kaisetsu ume, estimated to be over 670 years old. Over time, the site has inspired poets such as Sasaki Nobutsuna (佐佐木信綱), who composed tanka verses (see page 65) here, weaving literature into the presence of the blossoms.

OTHER JAPANESE APRICOT BLOSSOM SITES

Beyond the Three Great Ume Groves of Kanto described above, there are many other celebrated locations across Japan where Japanese Apricot blossoms can be enjoyed.

ATAMI UME GARDEN (熱海梅園), ATAMI CITY, SHIZUOKA PREFECTURE (JANUARY TO MARCH*)

Opened in 1886, Atami Ume Garden is an urban park known as one of Japan's earliest-blooming Japanese apricot spots. Spanning about 4 hectares (10 acres) along a river, the garden is home to nearly 470 Japanese apricot trees, of around 60 varieties, including some that are more than 100 years old. The annual Atami Ume Blossom Festival, held from January to March, celebrates the early arrival of the blossoms, marking the first sign of spring.

TANIGAWA UME GARDEN (谷川梅林), TACHIBANA TOWN, FUKUOKA PREFECTURE (LATE FEBRUARY*)

Considered one of Kyushu's three most famous ume gardens, Tanigawa Ume Garden features around 20,000 white Japanese apricot trees that cover the slopes. The Yume Tachibana Viewing Festival is held during peak bloom in late February, lasting for a limited number of days. This festival often includes traditional Japanese performing arts and cultural performances. Since Japanese apricot producers privately own the grove, it is open to the public only during the festival, making the experience even more special.

ANOU UME GROVE (賀名生梅林), GOJO CITY, NARA PREFECTURE (LATE FEBRUARY TO MARCH*)

Anou Ume Grove is one of Nara's most renowned ume destinations, with around 20,000 trees covering the hillsides. Japanese apricot viewing here dates back more than 700 years, with records of noblemen composing Japanese poetry under its blossoms. Tucked away in a remote part of Japan, this grove offers a serene retreat, ideal for those seeking a slower pace.

NANAORE UME GARDEN (七折梅園), TOBE TOWN, EHIME PREFECTURE (LATE FEBRUARY TO EARLY MARCH*)

With 16,000 Japanese apricot trees of around 30 varieties in shades of white and pink, Nanaore Ume Garden is one of Shikoku Island's highlights for apricot viewing. The hillside is filled with fragrance and colour, accompanied by the call of the Japanese bush warbler (uguisu), a traditional messenger of spring. The annual Nanaore Ume Festival enhances the experience with local food and cultural events.

> **The timing of blooming varies each year depending on climate conditions. These dates are general guidelines.*

A MOMENT OF REFLECTION

As you imagine the Japanese Apricot blossoms – braving the chilly air, blooming earlier than most – consider how resilience often shows itself in our own lives. We may think of resilience only in grand terms, yet it is often found in the subtle decisions we make every day.

Take a moment to recall a time when you showed courage, even in a small way.

Perhaps it was navigating a career path that aligned with your values, saying yes to an opportunity that stretched you, speaking out for something you believed in, or simply dedicating time to pause and refocus, despite the world urging you to move too quickly. These moments, though easy to overlook, are breadcrumbs of our own perseverance that deserve to be remembered and celebrated.

Just as the ume blossoms remind us that magnificence is built through the cold, may you honour the resilience already within you – the strength that has carried you this far, and will continue to help you bloom.

REFLECTION QUESTION

In what ways might you allow yourself to adapt, soften or take on new forms to stay resilient in the seasons of your own life?

UMEBOSHI (THE PICKLED UME): APRICOT BLOSSOM IN JAPANESE CUISINE

Umeboshi (梅干し), the pickled ume, is one of Japan's most representative and beloved culinary condiments. Made from ripe ume fruits that are pickled with salt and sun-dried before being stored, umeboshi are often enjoyed in small quantities with rice, either in an onigiri rice ball or a bento box. While there are various versions of umeboshi, they are traditionally known to be sour and salty.

Beyond their distinctive flavour, umeboshi have long been appreciated for their health benefits in Japanese traditional medicine. Rich in citric acid, they are believed to support digestion, combat fatigue and restore balance after physical or emotional strain. Even today, they remain a symbol of vitality, a reminder that preservation and strength are closely tied to what we fuel our bodies with.

Umeboshi continue to be a part of daily life in Japan. They can be found in supermarkets, restaurants and bento boxes across the country, with regional variations offering unique flavours and levels of saltiness or sweetness. If you have not tried them yet and have an Asian market nearby, it's worth checking to see if they are available. Umeboshi have a unique taste and are a delicacy that has nourished generations.

The ume reminds us that resilience is not only about endurance, but also adaptability. Whether admired as blossoms, used in medicine or preserved as food, it shows that strength can take many forms – softening, transforming and sustaining over time. Just as the Japanese apricot turns from flower to fruit to nourishment, we too can learn to adapt in ways that sustain our spirit.

PRACTICE: A TEA RITUAL FOR RESILIENCE

The versatility of ume blossoms reminds us that resilience is not about being rigid, but about adapting – finding strength in beauty, in nourishment or in healing, depending on what is needed in the moment.

Inspired by this tradition, you are invited to create a tea ritual as a way of nurturing resilience through everyday care. A cup of tea may seem simple, yet it can become a mindful act of building strength when approached with presence and intention.

Step 1: Choose your tea with care

If available, you may wish to try ume blossom tea, which can often be found in Asian supermarkets or speciality tea shops. Its floral aroma and gentle taste carry the essence of spring. If you cannot find it, select another herbal tea that feels nourishing to you – perhaps ginger for warmth, chamomile for calm or peppermint for relaxation. Let your choice reflect what you most need in this season of your life.

Step 2: Prepare with awareness

As the water heats, listen to the sound of the kettle, notice the rising steam and feel the warmth beginning to spread through your surroundings. While you prepare the water, take your time as you are already practising patience and presence – two qualities of resilience.

Step 3: Drink slowly and mindfully

Once your cup of tea is ready, find a soothing place to enjoy it – perhaps your cosy living room or an outdoor area with fresh air. Trust your instincts to guide you to a location that feels right. Hold the cup in both hands and – with each sip – notice the warmth moving through your body, as though it is carrying strength to every part of you. Allow yourself to fully enjoy this experience by paying attention to your senses, enjoying the aroma, taste, texture, sight and any sounds surrounding you.

Step 4: Reflect as you drink

Ask yourself gently:

When was the last time I offered myself care in a small but meaningful way?

What does my body or mind need most today to feel grounded and steady?

How can I create small, nourishing pauses in daily life that strengthen my resilience over time?

Step 5: Close with gratitude

When you finish your tea, take a moment to express gratitude – for the warmth of the cup, the nourishment it provided and the reminder that even small rituals over time can build strength.

This ritual goes beyond the act of drinking tea itself. When we create moments of honouring ourselves in the midst of life's challenges, we are strengthening our resilience. Just as ume blossoms embody resilience by blooming against the cold, so we too can find ways to care for ourselves in difficult seasons – calmly, confidently and with grace.

SUGAWARA NO MICHIZANE, THE GOD OF LEARNING & HIS LOVE FOR UME BLOSSOMS

When exploring the cultural and spiritual importance of ume blossoms in Japan, we cannot forget the fascinating story of Sugawara no Michizane (菅原道真, 845–903), who was renowned as a scholar, politician and poet. Michizane's life shows how resilience can be shaped through hardship, loyalty and transformation. His story has been told for over a thousand years and remains deeply tied to the ume blossom.

The Scholar and the Poet

Born in Kyoto, Michizane quickly gained recognition for his exceptional intellect and skill in Chinese literature. His sensitivity to nature and poetry appeared early; it is said that at the age of five, he wrote a poem about his love for the ume blossom, capturing its fragrance and beauty in his verse. He rose to prominence in the imperial court as an advisor to Emperor Uda, holding important positions in the government. Yet his success stirred rivalries. In 901, he was falsely accused of treason, stripped of his titles and exiled from Kyoto to Dazaifu (太宰府) in Kyushu, Japan southwestern main island, far from the advanced world of the city that was the capital of Japan at that time.

Exile and the Flying Ume

Life in exile was harsh. Michizane lived without income, grieved the loss of his honour and endured the challenging conditions of Dazaifu. It was during this time that the legend of the *tobi-ume* (飛梅, flying ume) was born. Before leaving Kyoto, Michizane is said to have composed a farewell poem to the ume tree he loved in his garden, expressing his hope that though he would be gone, its blossoms would not forget to bloom and release their fragrance in the spring.

According to legend, the tree could not bear to be parted from its master and flew overnight to Dazaifu, where it took root at the site where the Dazaifu Tenmangū Shrine (太宰府天満宮) was later built. Today, this tree is considered a sacred tree or *goshinboku* (御神木) and still stands within the precincts of Dazaifu Tenmangū. This variety of ume blossom, called *irotamagaki* (色玉垣), is the first to bloom in the shrine's grounds, flowering in the chill of winter, a symbol of perseverance and loyalty. Today, around 6,000 ume trees – made up of 200 varieties – are found in the shrine's sacred garden. Whether taken as history or folklore, the beloved story shares a principle of Japanese culture: that bonds of devotion and determination can endure even under the weight of adversity, sometimes exceeding our expectations of what is possible.

From Exile to Kami

Michizane died in exile, but his story did not end there. After his death, Kyoto was struck by storms and lightning, which many saw as signs of his restless spirit. In response, he was deified as Tenjin-sama (天神様), the Shinto *kami* (spirit) of learning, poetry and scholarship.

Shrines dedicated to Tenjin, known as *Tenmangū* (天満宮), were established across Japan. Today, there are thousands, and Dazaifu Tenmangū in Fukuoka is one of the head shrines. Each year in February, on the anniversary of Michizane's death, the shrine honours his love of ume blossoms: priests wear ume branches, shrine maidens (called *miko* 巫女) perform the Dance of the Flying Ume (*tobi-ume no mai* 飛梅の舞) and visitors come to admire the flowers that bloom in his memory. Even the shrine's crest or *shinmon* (神紋) is the *baika-mon* (梅花紋), a stylized ume blossom motif unique to Dazaifu, furthering the connection and symbolism of this story.

Rituals of Care and Community

Michizane's story is preserved through local traditions. A popular speciality sold in Dazaifu is *umegae-mochi* (梅ヶ枝餅), a rice cake stamped with an ume blossom design. It gets its name from the story of an elderly woman who, hearing that Michizane had little to eat, offered him mochi and gave it to him skewered on an ume blossom branch. Today, these treats are an essential part of the shrine experience, reminding us of the importance of community support in nurturing resilience.

The tale of Sugawara no Michizane – a transformation from disgraced exile to Tenjin-sama, the God of Learning – is an example of how hardship can, over time, be turned into resilience and an enduring spirit.

PRACTICE: EXPRESS YOUR RESILIENT SOUL WITH CREATIVE WRITING THROUGH TANKA

In the essence of the Japanese apricot blossom's resilience, you are invited to create your own tanka poem. *Tanka* (短歌), which means 'short song' or 'short poem', is a form of classical Japanese poetry, often composed while flower viewing. Tanka offers a concise yet eloquent way to express both personal reflection and the beauty of nature.

For this practice, let the themes of resilience, perseverance or the serene courage of the Japanese apricot blossoms inspire your tanka. The words you choose might reflect your own journey, or perhaps capture the presence of nature around you.

FINDING INSPIRATION

Take a notebook with you when you spend some serene time in nature. If you are fortunate to discover Japanese apricot blossoms in season, sit with them and observe their presence. If not, notice which flowers grow around you, especially those that emerge in less-than-ideal conditions. This can be a wonderful way to get to reconnect with your environment, and these blooms can remind us that resilience exists everywhere.

You can also lean into your sense of smell – Japanese apricot blossoms have long been admired for their fragrance. A particular scent can bring forth memories, feelings or states of mind with surprising immediacy.

You are now invited to reflect on your own life. Think back to a moment when you showed courage, resilience or perseverance – whether in a small daily choice, a difficult decision or a time you kept going despite hardship. These lived experiences can serve as seeds for your tanka, offering authenticity and depth.

GUIDELINES FOR WRITING YOUR TANKA:

- Begin by writing down words, phrases or images that surface as you reflect – sounds, sensations or emotions. Let sentences flow freely at first without worrying about syllable counts. The words do not need to rhyme.
- Then begin shaping these ideas into the 5–7–5–7–7 form, where the first line has 5 syllables, the second 7, the third 5, and the final two lines have 7 syllables each.
- When your poem feels complete, read it aloud. Notice how it flows. Are there words that could be shifted or refined to capture your intent more clearly?
- Finally, consider writing your finished tanka neatly on a piece of paper. Reading it aloud to yourself – or sharing it with a friend – can be a grounding way to bring your reflection into the world.

Here's an example written by me:

On a crisp, cold day
There lies an ume blossom
Still yet to open
Yet, she knows, with certainty
Her time will come soon to bloom

The practice of tanka is not about perfection but about expressing something genuine within the structure of the form. Paradoxically, the limitations can deepen creativity and clarity, helping you uncover truths that might not have been apparent otherwise.

PRACTICE: UME VISUALIZATION – PLANTING YOUR SEED OF RESILIENCE

This guided visualization invites you to connect with the strength of the ume blossom, blooming through the sharpness of winter. As you go through this practice, you will be reminded of your own capacity to expand and flourish, even in challenging conditions.

THE VISUALIZATION

Find a quiet space. Sit or lie down comfortably. Close your eyes gently, and bring your attention to your breath. Inhale slowly through your nose, feeling the fresh air energize your body. Exhale through your mouth, releasing any heaviness you may be carrying. Take a few more full breaths, allowing your body to arrive fully in this moment.

Now, imagine yourself standing outdoors in the stillness of late winter. The air around you is crisp and cool, almost sharp against your skin. You feel the quietness of the season – the bare branches, the soft colours of the earth and the gentle weight of the season's pause.

At the same time, as you look around, you see signs of spring. You notice a circle of stunning ume trees surrounding you. You look closer at a dark pink ume tree, and see its delicate petals unfurling, ever so slowly, but ever so surely. You then notice that the surrounding ume trees, in shades of white to crimson, are also starting to bloom. A sweet fragrance fills the air, and while the trees are yet to fully bloom, this beginning fills you with a strong, meaningful sense of hope.

With each breath, imagine the strength of these blossoms flowing into you. Feel it entering your chest, settling into your heart as a small but powerful seed of energy. This seed lives within you, representing your own inner strength – the ability to bloom through challenge, to persevere with grace.

As you breathe in, feel this energy expanding, spreading warmth through your body. As you breathe out, feel your body grounding into the earth, reminding you that you are supported. The blossom within you grows brighter with each breath, an emblem of your resilience.

With your hand on your chest, feeling this emblem, silently repeat this affirmation to yourself:

'I am blooming.'

Feel each word deeply and surely.

Take a few more breaths in this space, feeling the courage of the ume blossoms around you mirrored by the strength blossoming within you.

When you feel ready, slowly wiggle your fingers and toes and return to your body. Slowly open your eyes, carrying with you the resilience of the ume – a reminder that even in stillness and challenge, you have the strength to bloom.

CHAPTER WRAP-UP

As our chapter on Japanese Apricot blossoms comes to a close, take a moment to notice the seed of resilience that has been felt within you. It may be a realization of what needs to shift in your life to feel more adaptable, a memory of courageous action you once took or a feeling of confidence that you can meet life's upcoming challenges. Whatever has come to the surface, let it serve as a reminder that even when conditions are not ideal, we each hold the strength to nurture ourselves, to bloom and to persevere.

The Japanese apricot blossoms teach us that resilience is not a single act of strength, but a continual practice that builds over time. Each time we intentionally reconnect with our inner core, we strengthen our ability to keep going. When this stability feels distant, which it will most likely do at some point, you can return to the practices and reflections in this chapter – anchoring yourself in the beauty, scent and versatility of the ume blossoms as a reminder of your own capacity to adapt and thrive.

In the next chapter, we turn to momo, the peach blossom – vibrant, energetic and full of life. Where ume teaches us the courage of perseverance, momo reminds us of the joy and playfulness that paint our lives with vibrant moments.

CHAPTER 3

MOMO

桃

PEACH BLOSSOMS

Reclaiming Your Childlike Joy
and Sense of Play

MOMO 桃
Peach Blossoms

When I was growing up, my mother would tell me stories about how I never seemed to stop moving when I was little. She would smile as she described how I would spend entire days singing songs I had made up, dancing around our living room and making it my mission to express myself creatively to make my grandparents laugh. I was an endless ball of energy and creativity, full of laughter, carefree and easy-going.

As I got older, however, I began to dismiss those stories. I remember once almost annoyingly telling my mother that I wasn't that same person anymore – that I needed to be serious, to study hard and to prepare for a successful career. Like many of us, I thought that growing up meant being responsible, efficient and productive, and that spontaneity and being carefree were things of the past. I progressed in my adult life behind this serious shield I had put up for myself, only to be left with a sense of emptiness, that I had little to show for who I was as a person, despite following what I thought I had to do to be a responsible adult.

As a coach working with various clients, I have come to believe that my experience was not unique. I began to realize how easily many of us lose touch with that unguarded part of ourselves, the part that feels bursts of light and joy in simple acts of self-expression.

The peach blossom reminds us of this side of ourselves. It invites us to remember that joy and play are not things to discard; they are essential to our wellbeing. Just as the Japanese apricot blossoms taught us the power of resilience through winter's challenging chill, peach blossoms symbolize vitality and a sense of playfulness. Typically blooming between the Japanese apricot and the cherry blossoms, they are a burst of energy.

In Japan, peach blossom has long been associated with vitality, kindness and the power to ward off misfortune. In this chapter, we will explore its symbolism in Japanese culture, from its role in seasonal festivals to its traditional ties to folklore. We will also explore how it is linked to Japan's appreciation of *ki* (気) or energy, and the lessons it can teach us about managing energy with intention. Through folktales such as the story of Momotarō, or Peach Boy (see page 112), as well as traditional hands-on activities and crafts, we can reflect on the joy having fun brings and rediscover what it means to reconnect with our inner child. The part of us that still wants to dance, laugh and create for no reason other than that it feels good.

May the lessons of the peach blossom remind you that play is not something we had to leave in our childhood but is an essential life force – one that we can reclaim, that enlivens the spirit by giving us energy and connects us back to our most authentic selves.

HANAKOTOBA – THE FLOWER LANGUAGE OF MOMO

The flower meanings associated with peach blossoms in Japan are *kidate-no-yosa* (気立ての良さ), someone with a kind heart and consideration for others, along with *tenkamuteki* (天下無敵), which means 'to be invincible'. When brought together with the peach blossom's playful, joyous symbolism, these meanings invite us to pause and reflect. Perhaps when we allow ourselves to express childlike joy in our lives, we discover an inner strength that feels invincible, while also letting our natural kindness shine. When we realize that reconnecting with joy can also empower us to be kinder to others, we live from our soul. Take a moment to let this wisdom settle within you.

Reflection Question: When was the last time you felt a sense of pure, childlike joy? How did you relate to those around you while holding this feeling? Did it allow your natural kindness to flow more freely towards others?

WHEN DO PEACH BLOSSOMS BLOOM?

The peach blossoms begin to bloom from mid-March through to the end of April, depending on the region and climate. Like other spring blossoms, their bloom moves gradually northwards across the Japanese archipelago. Peach blossoms typically open after the apricot and just before the cherry, bridging the force of winter's end with the joy of spring's arrival.

If we look at Japan's traditional calendar, time was once divided into 72 micro-seasons (*shichijūni kō* 七十二候), each lasting about five days and reflecting subtle shifts observed in nature and seasonal rituals, from the frogs beginning to croak to the salmon swimming upstream. One of these, observed around 10 to 14 March, is called *momo hajimete saku* (桃始笑), meaning 'when the peach blossoms begin to bloom'.

Language has a way of carrying ancestral wisdom across generations. I find this expression deeply heart-warming. In Japanese, the character 笑 (*wara*), meaning 'to smile', was also used back in the day to describe blossoms opening. When I imagine my ancestors choosing this phrasing, I sense two messages. First, I can picture the smiles that the blooming peach blossoms brought to their faces. And second, I feel a reminder of how smiling, like blooming, is a natural part of life that we should appreciate and incorporate into our lives.

WHAT DO MOMO BLOSSOMS LOOK LIKE?

Of all Japan's spring blossoms, momo blossoms are often said to be the hardest to distinguish. Their form sits delicately between the rounded petals of the Japanese apricot (*ume*) and the heart-shaped tips of the cherry (*sakura*). Yet, if you look closely, there are a few characteristics that make this blossom unique. The petals have pointed tips and will flower alongside fresh, green leaves that appear simultaneously. The base of each branch typically holds two flowers which bloom in different directions.

Momo blossoms are most commonly seen in hues of pink, from the palest blush to bright shades, but some varieties bloom in white or vivid red. Like the Japanese apricot, peach trees are generally divided into two groups:

- ***Hana-momo*** (花桃): Cultivated for flower viewing, admired for the magnificence of its flowers.
- ***Mi-momo*** (実桃): Grown for their fruit and harvested from June onwards; enjoyed fresh or in sweets and preserves.

Among the flower-viewing varieties, several have long been admired in Japan for their character and beauty:

- ***Yaguchi*** (矢口): A soft pink, double-flowered variety often associated with *Hinamatsuri* (Girls' Day), used to decorate homes during the Peach Festival as a wish for happiness and good fortune.

- ***Kikumomo*** (菊桃): This variety is known for its slender petals, which resemble Japanese chrysanthemums. It produces deep crimson, double-layered flowers. As it blooms later than other varieties, it is often celebrated as one of the last momo blossoms of the season, extending the enjoyment of the blooming period.

- ***Genpei*** (源平): A captivating variety, where three colours of blossom – red, white and red-white varicoloured – bloom together on a single tree.

Each variety expresses its own unique personality – some are bold and bright, while others are soft and delicate. Even by just looking at the varieties, we can sense the abundance of joy, taking many forms to bloom.

PEACH BLOSSOM SPOTS IN JAPAN

Peach blossom viewing may not be as mainstream as cherry or Japanese apricot blossom viewing, but Japan still offers beautiful locations to enjoy this springtime event. The sites listed below offer a refreshing contrast to busy urban streets, inviting you into quieter settings where time may seem to move more slowly, allowing moments of pause. Coinciding with the gathering of peach blossoms, you will see that many of these areas host local festivals, community gatherings and opportunities to slow down and experience nature more intentionally and fully.

FUEFUKI PEACH BLOSSOM UTOPIA (笛吹桃源郷), FUEFUKI CITY, YAMANASHI PREFECTURE (LATE MARCH TO MID-APRIL*)

Fuefuki City is Japan's largest producer of peaches. Each spring, approximately 250,000 peach trees come into bloom, painting the landscape in soft pink colours often likened to what paradise or utopia might look like. There are various flower viewing spots available throughout the city, with one of the best vantage points being Yatsushiro Furusato Park, where you can enjoy a panoramic view of the city's peach fields. To celebrate their bloom, an annual Fuefuki Spring Festival is held from late March to mid-April, where visitors can explore designated viewing routes and local food stalls celebrating the season. Fuefuki City also has cherry blossom trees, making it an opportunity to appreciate both blossoms for their unique beauty.

HANAMOMO NO SATO (花桃の里), ACHI VILLAGE, NAGANO PREFECTURE (MID TO LATE APRIL*)

Found in the quiet Tsukikawa Onsen area of Achi Village, Hanamomo no Sato translates as 'the village of flowering peaches'. It is one of Japan's most picturesque hana-momo landscapes. More than 5,000 flowering peach trees line the paths, displaying a unique gradient of white, pink and red blossoms from the same type of tree. The nearby hot springs and clear night skies make it an ideal retreat for slowing down and reconnecting with nature. Visiting this area allows for a whole sensory experience – sight, scent, rest and stillness blend into one.

GŌDO STATION HANAMOMO (神戸駅花桃), MIDORI CITY, GUNMA PREFECTURE (LATE MARCH TO EARLY APRIL*)

Located in the mountainous, nature-filled rural prefecture of Gunma, Gōdo Station is a hidden gem. Part of the Watarase Keikoku Railway, this station has roughly 300 flowering peach trees along its tracks. During their blooming season, you can experience the peach blossoms while enjoying a slow-paced railway journey. There are no car parks at the station, so travellers are encouraged to take the train to visit, an intentional act of slowing down that lets the rhythm of the journey become part of the experience.

**Please check the local tourist websites to get the latest blooming timing, as this will vary slightly each year, depending on the climate and weather.*

A MOMENT OF REFLECTION

Each location has its own story and charm, reminding us that joy often emerges in moments of shared appreciation – in nature, within communities and through play.

In these places, we are not rushed, which can be such a gift. In our modern world, we often forget that we do not always have to try to find the quickest or most efficient way to do something. When we open up the space to slow down, it helps us get out of our minds and into our bodies and souls. It reminds us of the beauty of what makes us human, when we aren't thinking but 'being'. When we are 'being', we can hear what it is we really enjoy doing, and that feeling of joy will come to the surface.

As you imagine walking through these peach blossom landscapes at your own pace, ask yourself:

- *When was the last time I allowed myself to pause without rushing to the next thing?*
- *Where in my own life can I create space to simply savour – to breathe, to rest and to rediscover joy at my own pace?*
- *How can I create an environment that supports this feeling?*

Consider recording the answers to these questions in a journal. You can also share what has come up with a trusted friend or family member and explore with them how you can bring these thoughts into reality.

JAPAN'S TRADITIONAL SEASONAL FESTIVALS: THE GOSEKKU (五節句)

The *Gosekku* (五節句), or the five seasonal festivals, mark turning points in the seasons. Said to have originated in ancient China, these events take place during the transitional times of the year when people were believed to be more vulnerable to illness, as this was when 'evil spirits' could more easily enter their lives. To guard against this, communities and families came together to ward off the spirits and take good care of everyone's health. These ideas arrived in Japan during the Nara period (710–794) and were integrated with local customs and spiritual practices, which included preparing seasonal dishes, prayers and celebrations.

At their heart, these festivals are about gratitude and connection. Dishes are prepared not only for enjoyment but also as offerings, symbolizing wishes for good health, good harvests and connection with the spiritual or energetic elements around us. The festivals also serve as an opportunity for extended family, neighbours and friends to come together, strengthening a sense of collective harmony. While some of the spiritual elements may have diminished over time, these traditional events still hold meaning in Japan today. As modern life often limits our connection to nature, these rituals become reminders of alignment with the seasons.

All five festivals take place in months and on dates with odd numbers. In Japanese culture, odd numbers are considered lucky because they cannot be evenly divided, a symbol of wholeness and unbroken fortune. Traditionally, the Gosekku followed the lunar calendar, meaning the dates shifted according to the moon. Over time, these festivals became fixed to the Gregorian calendar, and are now observed on the same dates each year. Overleaf is a brief overview of the Gosekku before we turn our attention to the *Momo no Sekku* (Peach Festival) on page 109.

THE FIVE SEASONAL FESTIVALS OF JAPAN

7 JANUARY: JINJITSU / NANAKUSA NO SEKKU (人日 / 七草の節句)

Commonly known as *Nanakusa no Sekku* or the Festival of Seven Herbs, this day celebrates human life and longevity. Traditionally, people eat a warm rice porridge made with seven herbs to promote good health and recovery after the New Year's festivities.

3 MARCH: JŌSHI NO SEKKU / MOMO NO SEKKU (上巳 / 桃の節句)

This festival is known by two names: *Jōshi no Sekku* (上巳の節句), its historical name, and *Momo no Sekku* (桃の節句), the Peach Festival. The latter name came to be used as the festival began to coincide with the blossoming of peach trees, a symbol to ward off evil spirits. We will explore its deeper meaning on page 109.

5 MAY: TANGO NO SEKKU (端午の節句)

Now known as Children's Day, this festival celebrates the health and growth of children. Traditionally, iris leaves were used in baths as they were believed to possess medicinal properties, and they were hung in the home to ward off evil spirits. Today, colourful carp streamers (*koinobori*) are hung across Japan as symbols of strength and perseverance.

7 JULY: TANABATA NO SEKKU (七夕の節句)

The Star Festival is rooted in the story of two celestial lovers separated by the Milky Way. During this time, people are invited to write poems or wishes on colourful paper strips and hang them on bamboo branches. It's a summer celebration of romance and hope for the future.

9 SEPTEMBER: CHŌYŌ / KIKU NO SEKKU (重陽 / 菊の節句)

This festival honours the autumn harvest. The celebration includes the chrysanthemum (*kiku*), a flower believed to bring longevity and prevent misfortune. Families enjoy seasonal foods such as chestnuts and dishes made with edible chrysanthemums, offering prayers for good health as autumn begins.

While not everyone in Japan celebrates all five festivals today, their essence remains significant. The attention to seasonal foods in connection with energy and nature brings people together to acknowledge and share gratitude for the world's natural rhythm.

THE PEACH FESTIVAL: MOMO NO SEKKU (桃の節句)

The origins of this festival date back to the Heian period (794–1185), when court nobles used medicinal herbs to cleanse themselves of misfortune. This gradually transformed into the belief that negative energies could be transferred into dolls crafted from washi paper or plants. Known as *nagashibina* (流し雛), these dolls were sent gently floating down rivers to symbolically carry away misfortune, as water has long been a purifying and cleansing force in Japanese culture.

As the practice evolved, the floating paper dolls developed into the ornamental *hina-ningyō* (雛人形) we know today. Displays of dolls representing the emperor, empress, musicians and court attendants are arranged on a tiered platform. As these dolls can be expensive, they have traditionally been passed down as family heirlooms. The belief remains that the dolls serve as substitutes for people, absorbing misfortune on their behalf and protecting the wellbeing of those in the household, especially young girls. Peach blossom sprigs are also used as part of the decorations as they are said to have the power to ward off evil spirits.

Today, this day is known as *Hinamatsuri*, or Girls' Day. Families gather to celebrate the health, happiness and growth of their daughters, and the essence of femininity. The festival is accompanied by delicious dishes and drinks, such as *chirashi-zushi* (scattered sushi), *hina-arare* (sweet, multi-coloured, bite-sized rice crackers), and *shirozake* (sweet white sake). These delicacies include symbolic elements with thoughtful intentions behind them, including ingredients associated with good luck and cleansing beliefs. Beyond its protective feminine associations, the spirit of *Momo no Sekku* communicates a broader message of community. It reminds us to gather with our loved ones and reconnect with joy through shared rituals.

PRACTICE: CREATE AND CELEBRATE YOUR OWN NATURE FESTIVAL WITH LOVED ONES

Inspired by the Peach Festival (*Momo no Sekku*), this practice invites you to reconnect with joy through seasonal rituals and a sense of harmony. Let's create an intentional gathering that you can celebrate with your family, friends or chosen community that aligns with the natural rhythm around you.

REFLECT ON YOUR SEASONAL MEMORIES

Think back to a seasonal celebration or family ritual from your childhood or culture – perhaps a local festival or gathering that connected you with nature. If nothing comes to mind, that's perfectly fine. You can begin fresh by creating your own.

CHOOSE YOUR SEASON AND INTENTION

Look at which foods are in season where you live. You can visit a local market where you can talk with local producers, or explore seasonal local listings (for example, the National Trust in the UK). Choose an element that you are drawn to – perhaps a fruit, flower or scent, and let that become the symbol of your celebration.

DESIGN YOUR RITUAL

Create a simple act to mark the season. You might cook a dish using your seasonal ingredient of choice, display a flower that's in bloom, take a nature walk with loved ones or pause for gratitude before a meal. Keep it simple and intentional, and enjoy creating this ritual for yourself or with your loved ones. There are no right or wrong rituals – the purpose is to create an intentional connection that feels right for you.

SHARE AND CELEBRATE

Invite others to join you. It could be one person or many. Enjoy the act of slowing down, as well as sharing conversation, laughter and the simple act of being together. Let the moments of joy that will come naturally from these experiences sink in.

When we come together with others and nature through intentional rituals, we remind ourselves that joy is an energy that brings people together and nourishes our hearts.

THE FOLKTALE OF MOMOTARŌ (桃太郎) – THE PEACH BOY

The story of *Momotarō* (桃太郎), or Peach Boy, is one of Japan's most cherished folktales, one that nearly every child grows up hearing – a hero's journey filled with messages of courage, teamwork and kindness.

A long time ago, there was an elderly couple who lived in a quiet, remote village in Japan. Every day, the husband went to the mountains to collect firewood, and the wife went to the nearby river to wash their clothes. One day, the wife saw a giant peach floating towards her; she picked it up and took it home to show her husband. Just as they were about to open the peach, it split into two, and a baby boy emerged. Surprised yet overjoyed, the couple saw this as a blessing, as they had no children of their own. They named him Momotarō, a combination of *momo* (peach) and *tarō*, a common Japanese given name for a boy. Momotarō grew up kind-hearted, courageous, strong, and full of energy – a child who brought laughter and life into his parents' home.

One day, word spread that ogres (*oni* 鬼) from a distant island were coming to frighten the villagers and steal their treasures. Momotarō told his parents that he would go to the ogres' island to fight back and bring peace to the village. Though his parents were worried, they sensed his determination and gave him a sword for protection and *kibi-dango* (Japanese millet dumplings) for strength on his journey.

During his journey to the island, Momotarō met and recruited three animals to join him – a dog, a monkey and a pheasant – each agreeing to help in exchange for a share of his delicious dumplings. Together, they defeated the *oni* by using their individual strengths: the pheasant flew over the enemy to observe their defences, the monkey helped strategize and the dog protected the group with his loyalty. They returned home to the village with the stolen treasures, restoring peace and harmony.

The story of Momotarō represents the qualities of an energetic spirit symbolized by the peach itself. It also shows us what becomes possible when we live in alignment with this spirit – courageously facing our challenges and working for the good of others. It also reminds us that when we work as a team that respects and encourages everyone's unique strengths, amazing things happen.

What makes this story timeless is its connection to the spirit of childhood. Listening to the tale of Momotarō as a child, I vividly imagined a giant peach floating down the river, splitting in two, and Momotarō gathering his animal companions to defeat the mythical monsters. As adults, we may no longer live within fairy tales, but the imagination and playfulness that this story brings out are still alive within each of us.

PRACTICE: RECONNECTING WITH YOUR CHILDHOOD SELF

Inspired by the story of *Momotarō*, this practice invites you to reconnect with your childhood self. The part of you that found joy in imagination, creativity and play. The goal is not nostalgia but reconnection – to reclaim the energy and freedom that naturally reside within you.

---

1. **Recall your childhood moments**
   Think back to the activities, dreams or feelings that defined your early years. What did you love to do? How did you express yourself – through movement, creativity, nature or curiosity? What activities filled the days when you lost track of time? Did you play dress-up and role play? Or did you prefer to solve jigsaws and puzzles, or build racetracks for toy cars? Perhaps you were out in the playground enjoying the monkey bars and swings, or you enjoyed immersing yourself in the endless world of books.

   You may also find there were ways of expressing yourself that you wish you had done more of as a child, but for whatever reason could not. This, too, is part of your childhood self: something to honour and lean into.

   If memories feel distant, ask your family or close friends for stories about you as a child, or look through old photos to reconnect with that part of your life.

2. **Express your story**
   Choose a way to bring your childhood essence to life – something that reflects how you felt during that time. Allow yourself to do it imperfectly, with openness rather than self-judgement. You could:

- Write a short story of your childhood self (you can use the story of Momotarō as inspiration).
- What was your adventure?
- Who were your companions?
- What did you learn along the way?
- Write your story as if it were a children's book, including dialogue, actions and expressions.
- Draw or sketch your story as a picture book.
- Paint a childhood version of yourself that represents this story.
- Play or listen to music that brings you back to this period of your life.

3. **Share and reflect**
   When you are ready, read or show your creation to yourself and take a moment to sit with how it makes you feel. Then, if it feels right, share it with one or two people you trust – perhaps your family, partner or a close friend.

   Instead of focusing on your thoughts, notice how it feels to bring this part of you forwards again. Do you feel a sense of warmth and light emerging from within?

4. **Integrate your joy**
   Ask yourself: How might I bring a little more of this energy into my everyday life? Can I incorporate more of the creative and expressive activities that I used to enjoy as a child into my day-to-day life?

   List what that might look like for you now, and think of who in your circle you could invite to join you. You can absolutely do this on your own, but sharing it with someone you trust can make it lighter and more joyful to sustain.

This practice is a reminder that your childlike joy never disappears and lives within each of us.

This is your invitation to return.

When we remember how to play,
we remember how to live joyfully.

UNDERSTANDING KI (気): THE JAPANESE CONCEPT OF ENERGY

For us to understand the essence of joy, we must explore one of Japan's most fundamental and nuanced concepts: *ki* (気). *Ki* can be described as the energy and vitality that sustains all living things, including ourselves and the world around us.

While *ki* is often translated as 'energy', in Japan its concept and meaning are much more significant. It is not simply something mystical or supernatural that can be ignored; it reflects the fundamental ways we live, relate and connect within Japanese culture. That said, how can we understand something that is not always visible or tangible? To me, one of the best ways to understand *ki* is through language itself, almost as if it were a message from our ancestors.

In Japanese, countless words include 気, the *ki*, and together they reveal how naturally this concept is woven into daily life. Here are a few examples that offer a glimpse into how *ki* manifests in our everyday expressions:

- ***Genki*** (元気) means 'well' or 'healthy' and is used to ask someone 'How are you?' The first character, *gen* (元), means 'source' or 'foundation', so when we ask someone, 'Genki?', we are really asking, 'How is your foundational energy?'

- ***Kimochi*** (気持ち) means 'feelings' or 'emotions'. Here, *mochi* (持ち) means 'to hold', so the word literally expresses how we hold or carry our energy within.

- ***Tenki*** (天気) means 'weather', where *ten* (天) refers to 'heaven' or 'sky'. The weather, then, is seen as the sky's energy – a reflection of nature's changing moods.

These are just a few examples among hundreds, but they illustrate something essential: that energy in Japan is not separate from daily life. Whether we talk about health, emotion or nature, *ki* connects all of them.

There are also expressions that show how *ki* shapes our worldview:

- ***Yamai wa ki kara*** (病は気から) means 'illness begins with the spirit'. It is a reminder that the state of our heart and energy influences our wellbeing.

- ***Iki tōgō suru*** (意気投合する) means 'to be in perfect harmony'. This can describe deep resonance between friends, colleagues or partners where you share energetic alignment.

- ***Kyoshin heiki*** (虚心平気) means 'to calm the heart and mind by letting go of doubts and distrust'. Here, *heiki* means 'to steady the spirit', while *kyoshin* refers to a mind free of clutter and a clear, unburdened heart.

When I reflect on these words, I realize that most Japanese people aren't consciously thinking about energy in a spiritual sense, yet it is present in how we speak, act and relate to one another. Growing up in Japan, this was part of everyday life. We notice whether someone's *ki* feels high, low or uneasy, by reading the atmosphere (an expression we refer to as *kūki o yomu* (空気を読む), or sensing the energy of a room before speaking.

Even if you don't subscribe to spiritual ideas, I invite you to reflect on this: what drains your energy and what replenishes it? Each of us, no matter where we come from, can feel the shift between when our *ki* is low and when it flows freely.

Joy is one of life's greatest energy chargers. It's that warm, expansive feeling that fills you from within – a quiet aliveness that makes you feel connected to the present moment. When we nurture joy, we nourish our *ki*.

As you begin to notice your own energy, start paying attention to how it flows through your day: in your breath, conversations, creative moments and pauses. The Japanese understanding of *ki* reminds us that energy exists not only within us, but also in our connections with others, with nature and with life itself.

When we learn to tend to our *ki* with awareness and care, we begin to cultivate a lifestyle that feels more balanced, more harmonious – and ultimately, more full of joy.

PRACTICE: GENKI ENERGY LIST

Now that we've opened our awareness to *ki*, use this practice as a way to lean into the feeling of energy and being alive that joy brings. This is your invitation to cultivate a more *genki* lifestyle every day.

A simple list can be a powerful tool, a way to gain clarity on what it is in your life that truly charges your joy-energy batteries. **There's no need to try everything; instead, begin with one or two ways of inviting more energy into your day that you feel naturally drawn to.**

Test them out and notice how your *ki* feels afterwards. Do you feel lighter, warmer or more energized? If the answer is yes, see how you might incorporate even only 10 to 15 minutes of that activity into the week ahead. Start small – remember that consistency builds lasting change.

If you feel unsure where to start, try reflecting on this question:

'If I had a weekend completely to myself, free from responsibilities, how would I spend my time?'

Let this start your joy energy engine. You may also want to reflect on the following questions:

- Who in your life brings you joy?
- What environments elevate your energy?
- What activities make you feel warm or charged, or make you laugh?

Rather than forcing answers, give yourself permission to slow down. Leave space for boredom – because in stillness, joy often finds its way back to us.

Here are a few examples from my own Genki Energy List:

- Morning walks with my husband
- Eating homemade, nourishing meals made by my mum
- Singing karaoke with my sister
- Baking and trying out new recipes
- Nature walks with my friends
- Video calls with friends abroad
- Appreciating the changing colours of the autumn leaves
- Walking along the River Thames and watching the boats and waves
- Trying my husband's homemade sourdough bread
- Sauna sessions
- Writing handwritten letters and cards to family and friends
- Japanese calligraphy intention-writing sessions in the morning

Write out your own Genki Energy List and keep it somewhere visible. Come back to it whenever your energy feels low or your days feel heavy. Choose one thing from your list – even something small – and bring it into your day.

JAPAN'S CONNECTION TO WORKING WITH OUR HANDS

Let's imagine for a moment how people in the past spent their day. I picture them doing a variety of activities throughout their waking hours, with a common theme of moving their bodies and working with their hands. Tasks such as cooking, gardening, sewing and cleaning not only required physical movement, but also offered people opportunities to connect with the world around them and be creative. In sharp contrast, today our hands spend much of their time tied to devices. That may be typing on a keyboard, using a smartphone or switching between streaming shows on the television.

Using our hands for screen-based tasks instead of engaging in hands-on activities can sometimes leave us feeling disconnected from the world around us. I believe this is a key reason why joy is missing from many of our lives today.

In Japan, the tradition of working and creating with one's hands has long been respected and deeply valued. Let's see what lessons we can take away from this tradition and how to incorporate them into our lives today.

Japanese Traditional Crafts

Hundreds of traditional crafts are practised across Japan, often shaped by the resources and character of each region – whether that be pine forests that provide soot for ink, a type of bamboo for whisks that thrives in a specific climate, or clay from local mountains to be made into ceramics. These crafts have been passed down through generations of artisans, typically within families or through apprenticeships, where both the techniques and spirit are slowly inherited over time.

Some crafts have gained global recognition in recent years – such as kintsugi, the art of repairing broken pottery with lacquer and gold, celebrating the beauty of what has cracked or changed rather than hiding it. Yet kintsugi represents only a small glimpse into Japan's rich and expansive craft heritage. Here are a few examples of traditional crafts that continue to be respected in Japan today.

ARITA-YAKI / IMARI-YAKI (有田焼 / 伊万里焼), ARITA TOWN & IMARI CITY, SAGA PREFECTURE

Japanese porcelain, known for its bright white base and vibrant painted designs, originated in Arita during the 17th century. It was later transported from the port of Imari to markets around the world, which is why the terms Arita ware and Imari ware have often been used interchangeably. Today, pieces made in the Arita area are known as Arita-yaki, while those made in the Imari area are known as Imari-yaki. Blending artistry with durability, the wares made here today bring the spirit of craftsmanship into Japanese homes and shared meals every day.

TAKAYAMA CHASEN (高山茶筌), TAKAYAMA, IKOMA CITY, NARA PREFECTURE

Handmade tea whisks have been made from local bamboo in the Takayama area of Ikoma City, Nara Prefecture, for more than 500 years. Using a small knife and hand-carving techniques, the craftspeople create more than 100 varieties of these tea ceremony utensils for specific occasions. They are made by a few Chasen-masters who continue to produce the highest-quality pieces using their traditional techniques.

SUZUKA-ZUMI (鈴鹿墨), SUZUKA CITY, MIE PREFECTURE

This ink, crafted by burning local pine to create fine soot, has supported Japanese calligraphy and ink painting for more than 1,300 years. Artisans mix the soot with natural glue, knead it by hand and shape it into ink sticks, which are then slowly dried and matured. The result of this labour-intensive process is ink known for its depth of colour and smooth flow. There is only one workshop that continues this Suzuka sumi tradition in Japan: Shinseidō in Suzuka City.

ECHIZEN-YAKI (越前焼), ECHIZEN TOWN, FUKUI PREFECTURE

One of Japan's Six Ancient Kilns, Echizen-yaki has a rich history going back around 850 years. The pottery made here is often fired without glaze, letting the elegance of the fine clay body shine through. Today, it is used to make sake bottles, jars, bowls and cups. Its wares are celebrated for their simplicity, durability and delicate texture shaped by the fine clay of the region.

While these are just a few of the traditional crafts Japan has to offer, a respect for nature's resources and a deep appreciation for creating with one's hands can be felt in all of them. Yet, Japan is not immune to the challenge of finding people who want to learn such skills and keep them alive. Let's take a moment to appreciate the work of artisans and reintegrate the practice of working with our hands into our lives. By doing so, we can preserve traditional techniques and learn wisdom from the past. Working with our hands connects us to ourselves and the world around us.

Traditional Arts of Japan – *Dentō Sandō* (伝統三道)

Alongside these crafts, Japan also has many traditional arts. Among them are the forms known as *Dentō Sandō* (伝統三道). Rather than focusing on producing crafts, these ancient art forms teach us how to live with intention throughout life's journey.

The three traditional arts are:

- ***Sadō*** (茶道): the Japanese tea ceremony
- ***Shodō*** (書道): Japanese calligraphy
- ***Kadō*** (華道): Japanese flower arrangement

Each art form includes the character 道 (*dō*), meaning 'the way', combined with another character representing the discipline itself – 茶 for 'tea', 書 for 'writing' and 華 for 'flower'. By practising these arts, we learn to be more present, more intentional and more aware in our everyday lives.

The many teachings within each art form offer insight into how we can do this. Here is a glimpse into what we can learn from each one.

FROM *SADŌ*: *ICHIGO ICHIE* (一期一会)

A four-character idiom meaning 'one encounter, one meeting'. Originating from the Japanese tea ceremony, *ichigo ichie* reminds us that each encounter is unique and will never be repeated, and that every meeting deserves our full attention. When we recognize that this truth extends beyond the tearoom to all of our interactions, we can approach each moment with greater intention and gratitude.

FROM *SHODŌ*: *MUSHIN* (無心)

Translated as 'mind of no mind', *mushin* is the state one strives for while practising Japanese calligraphy – free from thought, judgement or emotion, and completely present in movement. Paradoxically, to think of being in this state is to step out of it. Calligraphy acknowledges this and teaches us to focus on the movement of the brush rather than the outcome, allowing flow to arise naturally. It reminds us that presence does not always require stillness; it can be found through rhythm and motion.

FROM *KADŌ*: THE BEAUTY OF SUBTRACTION

The Japanese art of flower arrangement teaches the importance of space. While other floral-arrangement traditions may focus on abundance, *kadō* highlights beauty through subtraction, how less can be more. By doing so, the true essence of nature – and of ourselves – has room to breathe. This teaching reminds us that even outside of flower arranging, there is wisdom in subtracting from our lives, as this frees up space for things to naturally appear.

These arts teach us that joy often emerges from returning to our senses rather than rushing ahead: noticing the preciousness of each gathering, the movement of the brush and the serene beauty in simplicity.

PERSONAL STORY

I have practised Japanese calligraphy for more than 25 years, starting at a young age thanks to my mother, who wanted me to have a way to connect with my culture. She has practised for more than 40 years and holds the title *shihan* (grand master instructor). She continues to remind me of one of the first lessons – *our writing never lies.*

While our minds and self-judgement can easily distort how we see ourselves, our calligraphy reflects our truth peacefully. Each stroke reveals our state of being, encompassing our energy, focus, emotions and inner balance – in a way that words often cannot. When I feel unsettled or distracted, it shows. When I am at ease, the brush flows effortlessly.

Some of my favourite calligraphy pieces are ones I initially disliked. Just after writing them, all I could hear were my harsh voices of self-criticism and doubt. Yet, when I returned to the same piece days or weeks later, I began to see it differently – not crowded by the strict words of criticism in my mind, but for what I saw on the paper. Through calligraphy, I've learned that beauty often reveals itself over time, and that our first reaction is not always the most accurate one.

This practice continues to remind me that joy and self-acceptance come from letting go of perfection and returning to presence – seeing ourselves, quite literally, as we are on the page. In this way, calligraphy, like play, becomes a mirror – a way to rediscover the joy of seeing ourselves with openness and curiosity.

ORIGAMI – THE ART OF PAPER FOLDING

Origami is said to have been introduced to Japan by Buddhist monks in the 7th century, and eventually became a popular way for children and families to express their creativity using only their hands and a single square of paper. The art of paper folding is still practised in Japan today, often in schools or as a family activity. A sequence of folds becomes a flower, an animal or an everyday object. The creations that can be made are virtually limitless – a beautiful reminder that we can each make something unique, even when starting from the same point.

Orizuru (折り鶴), the paper crane, holds a special place in Japan. Cranes are mythical symbols of longevity, vitality and devotion. A traditional practice tied to cranes is *senbazuru* (千羽鶴) – stringing together a thousand folded cranes to carry a heartfelt wish for peace, happiness or recovery from challenging times. It is often created collectively, bringing people together through shared intention and care. Senbazuru gained wider recognition in Japan and around the world through the story of Sadako Sasaki, a young girl from Hiroshima who began folding cranes as a wish for healing and peace after becoming ill from radiation exposure. Her story continues to resonate as a symbol of resilience and a wish for a more peaceful world.

If you pay attention, you will notice paper cranes across Japan, displayed in schools, temples and shrines, as well as at sporting events or in offices. Most people in Japan know how to fold a crane, a knowledge held close throughout life, linking generations through imaginative expression and shared memory. Working with our hands in this way reminds us that creativity, connection and joy are not separate. They grow through simple actions, done with heart and often shared with others.

PRACTICE: FOLDING A PAPER CRANE (OR ORIZURU 折り鶴)

Folding a paper crane is one of Japan's most cherished creative traditions. Now that we have explored the world of origami, you may wish to try folding one yourself. You can fold one not for perfection, but for the calm that comes from each fold.

In Japan, origami paper is often sold as square sheets in various colours and patterns, including traditional Japanese prints. One side is usually coloured and the other blank. These can be found in stationery stores throughout the country, as well as across the world. You can also easily find origami paper sets online. Alternatively, you can use an ordinary sheet of paper cut into a square.

If you're new to folding a paper crane, you can follow a simple step-by-step guide – many tutorials are available online or in beginner origami books. As you start, take a moment to breathe. Feel the texture of the paper in your hands. You are not here to perform, but to play.

You may also invite a friend, colleague or family member to join you in this practice. Welcome the quiet that comes while folding, as words may not be needed. Time spent together, doing something with your hands, can create its own form of connection and shared stillness.

When you finish making your paper crane, place it somewhere visible – a reminder to celebrate your creative joy.

CHAPTER WRAP-UP

As we close this chapter on peach blossoms, can you feel a childlike energy returning – a lightness that fills your heart? This chapter has been about bringing vibrancy back into your life, whether through seasonal festivals, reconnecting with childhood joy and *genki* energy, or working with your hands.

Peach blossoms invite us to keep hold of that joy and the energy it gives. Each time we choose to lean into it, we recharge. When life feels heavy – as it will at times – return to these pages to reignite your sense of play.

In the next chapter, we turn to sumomo – the Japanese plum blossom – humble, modest and quietly confident. Where momo teaches the vibrancy of life, sumomo reminds us that true confidence grows from being comfortable in yourself, for yourself.

CHAPTER 4

SUMOMO

李

JAPANESE PLUM BLOSSOMS

The Gift of Inner Confidence and Humility

SUMOMO 李
Japanese Plum Blossoms

In the language of flowers, the hanakotoba of sumomo – the Japanese plum – includes meanings such as 'misunderstanding' (*gokai* 誤解), 'independence' (*dokuritsu* 独立) and 'unpretentious elegance' (*kazaranai jōhinsa* 飾らない上品さ). Of these, misunderstanding has always stood out to me, as it touches on a subtle truth of being human. In my coaching work, people often tell me how misunderstood they feel – sometimes by their friends or family, sometimes in their workplace and sometimes throughout their lives. Perhaps you've felt this way too: when those around you didn't truly understand who you are or what you meant; when you said something with good intention that was taken differently; when your quietness was mistaken for being 'too shy' or 'aloof'; or when your honesty was perceived as being 'too direct' or 'opinionated'.

Almost everyone experiences this feeling of being unseen or misread at some point, yet it is rarely discussed. It can leave us questioning who we are or feeling the need to change ourselves to fit in. It can also manifest in many ways – perhaps through overcompensating and demanding that your needs be met, or on the other end of the spectrum, people-pleasing to the point of exhaustion. You might deny your emotional needs and appear stronger than you truly feel, or you might distance yourself from closeness, believing that no one will fully understand you.

These are delicate, challenging moments. The first step to working through them is to recognize how they are showing up in your life – a process that is never easy. Yet the sumomo reminds us that being misunderstood does not mean there is something wrong that needs 'fixing'. What if, instead, we took it as a sign that we are in the process of becoming more ourselves? A moment to pause and create an internal and external environment that aligns with who we truly are.

Welcome to the last of our four blossoms: the Japanese plum. This final bloom in oubaitori does not receive as much attention as the first three, and this fact becomes its own teaching – one of humility and self-confidence that grows not from external praise but from within.

As mentioned on page 14, both ume and sumomo are often translated as 'plum' in English, which can be confusing. In Japan, however, they are distinct blossoms and fruits with their own names, seasons and meanings. The ume blooms first, signalling the start of spring, while the sumomo follows afterwards, its fruit ripening as the season warms. This distinction reminds us that, much like the sumomo, we too can be easily mistaken for something or someone else if not looked at closely. Sometimes, what others misunderstand may simply mean they have not yet seen our full depth. The Japanese plum invites us to slow down, to look carefully and to appreciate quiet uniqueness – both in ourselves and in others.

This chapter will look a little different from the previous three. While we will touch lightly on the sumomo blossom's season and appearance, our focus will turn inwards – towards what this humble bloom teaches us about confidence, respect and the quiet strength of being at ease with who we are. Through reflections rooted in Japanese culture, we will explore how humility can coexist with strength and community, and how confidence grows from authenticity rather than comparison. May the lessons of the sumomo encourage you to welcome the beauty of being yourself, to nurture confidence from within, and to find grace in humility – trusting that your authentic self will shine through.

SYMBOLISM & SIGNIFICANCE OF THE PLUM BLOSSOM IN JAPAN

While the *sumomo* (李), or Japanese plum blossom, is sometimes mistaken for the other three blossoms of oubaitori, it is important to note that it is unique and distinct in its own beautiful way. The sumomo carries a specific charm, often overlooked among Japan's more famous blossoms, yet it holds a subtle strength and depth of essence.

The name sumomo is said to have come from the appearance of its fruit, which look similar to peaches but have a tarter flavour – *su* meaning 'sour' and *momo* meaning 'peach'. Its blossoms, too, are sometimes confused with those of other spring trees.

WHEN DO JAPANESE PLUM BLOSSOMS BLOOM?

The Japanese plum tree typically blooms from March to April. Its white flowers bloom before the leaves emerge, giving the branches a delicate and elegant appearance.

HANAKOTOBA – THE FLOWER LANGUAGE OF SUMOMO

This sense of mistaken identity ties into one of the *hanakotoba* – the flower language – of *sumomo*: 'misunderstanding' (*gokai*). While this word may at first sound negative, it can also be seen as a reflection of individuality. It represents those who may be misread or misunderstood, even though they hold a presence that is sincerely unique and stunning in their own way.

Other *hanakotoba* for *sumomo* include 'independence' (*dokuritsu*) and 'unpretentious elegance' (*kazaranai jōhinsa*). When we take time to understand something or someone beyond first impressions and preconceived notions, what often emerges is not confusion but clarity. These meanings together reflect the force of the *sumomo*: a stunning yet humble confidence that does not need to announce itself. Its elegance is found in its humility. It reminds us that confidence and humility can coexist, and that genuine beauty often reveals itself when no one is watching.

WHAT DO JAPANESE PLUM BLOSSOMS LOOK LIKE?

Each blossom has five rounded petals and forms clusters of three to five buds per node. Their flower stalks are longer than those of the ume or momo, and compared to the cherry blossom, the petals of sumomo are rounder, lacking the distinct notched tip that gives sakura its heart-shaped form.

These differences may seem small, but they hold a meaningful teaching. When we pay close attention, we begin to notice the distinct features that might otherwise go unseen and that make us all different. Just as the sumomo is often mistaken for something else, there are times in our lives when we, too, are not immediately understood. Yet, in both nature and life, when we take the time to see – to truly see – it allows us to appreciate the beauty that lies beneath first impressions.

PRACTICE:
TO SEE AND BE SEEN

The next time you step outside, take a slow breath and look closely at your surroundings. Notice one thing you may never have paid attention to before, perhaps the texture of a tree trunk, the form of a blooming flower, the design of a building or the rhythm of the wind.

This practice extends beyond nature. It is also about learning to see – authentically – the people and things around us. The beauty and the curse of being human is that we are remarkably skilled at processing information. Over time, this ability can turn into unconscious assumptions. We begin to move through life seeing what we *expect* to see, rather than what is actually there.

As we learned from the cherry blossoms, nothing in life is permanent. We are changing and evolving every day. Look in the mirror and take the time to see yourself for who you are today, in this very moment, not who you were yesterday, or who you think you should be.

Take a moment to watch someone dear to you – your partner, a friend or a family member – and truly look at them. Notice what is new: a subtle expression, a gesture or a different energy that may not have been there before. When we slow down enough to notice, we begin to see not only differences but depth.

Take your time with this practice. Begin with five minutes. Make the time to take in the delicate details as well as to simply observe. Pay attention to what you see without judgement. We are not here to analyse or assess, only to witness, to soak in what is present.

When you start to truly see yourself, others and the world around you, you begin to nurture understanding. In that act of seeing, something shifts. Presence deepens. Connection strengthens. This simple yet powerful act of awareness can create a ripple effect that touches far beyond what we can perceive.

JAPAN'S CONNECTION TO HUMILITY & INNER CONFIDENCE

In many ways, the spirit of the sumomo mirrors an element found across Japanese culture – that strength does not need to be loud, and confidence does not require recognition. In Japan, confidence often stems from humility, from the certainty of knowing who you are without needing to prove it.

Let's explore a few key cultural concepts that reflect this connection between humility and inner confidence.

Kenkyo (謙虚), meaning modesty or humility, is a virtue deeply ingrained in Japanese culture. To be kenkyo is to avoid overestimating one's ability or position, no matter how far one advances. It encompasses respect for others, openness to feedback and an ongoing commitment to learning. Kenkyo is not about self-denial, as it is sometimes understood to be. Instead, it emphasizes balance – the ability to sincerely receive praise while remaining grounded. When you embody kenkyo, you can appreciate your growth without arrogance, celebrate your team's efforts before your own and stay curious about how to improve.

This same balance is reflected in *bushidō* (武士道), the way of the Japanese warrior – an ethical and moral path that balances courage with restraint, and strength with self-discipline. Bushidō's philosophy not only guided warriors of the past but continues to shape everyday interactions. Among its virtues is *rei* (礼), or politeness, which reminds us that courtesy is not a superficial formality but an act of dignity. In practising respect for others, we strengthen our own integrity. Our actions and words become small yet meaningful expressions that build up our inner confidence over time.

Another cultural idea that echoes humility is *shoshin* (初心), meaning 'beginner's mind'. The word combines the characters for 'beginning' (*sho* 初) and 'heart' (*shin* 心), and refers to the curiosity, openness and humbleness we hold when starting something new. Shoshin has its roots in Buddhism, where it was originally expressed as *shohosshin* (初発心) – the initial awakening of the heart that seeks enlightenment. It reflects the moment one becomes aware of the desire to learn or grow, reminding us that the very act of wanting to understand is itself part of the path.

Shoshin was explored by Zeami Motokiyo (1363–1443), the classical Noh theatre actor and writer, in his work *Kakyō* (*A Mirror of the Flower*), in which he described the importance of maintaining a beginner's spirit throughout life. He outlined three lessons to embrace shoshin: To remember the aspiration and curiosity one had at the beginning, to carry that same spirit even as experience grows, and to continue learning and refining one's art in later life. Although these teachings were initially intended for Noh theatre, this idea has become widespread and is held as a guiding wisdom in Japan. When we remain humble, we can maintain our drive to learn and, in turn, grow in confidence.

These elements form the heart of a confidence that is grounded, graceful and dignified – a confidence much like the sumomo itself.

REFLECTION QUESTION: Where in your life can you cultivate a more shoshin way of being? Is there something you have practised for many years that has become routine? Think back to the time when you first began it. How did it feel? What inspired you? Take a moment to reconnect with that initial spark and the feeling of curiosity and wonder. How might you bring that energy into your life again?

Perhaps you can start something new, return to a forgotten hobby or simply approach the familiar with a beginner's spirit. Whatever it may be, let shoshin be your guide to humility.

RESPECT AS A MIRROR OF HUMILITY IN JAPAN

When I was growing up in Japan, respect was not something taught through lengthy explanations or loud statements. Instead, it was something I absorbed by watching how people moved through their everyday lives. I still remember waiting for my mum to come home one day. From our balcony, I saw her pause in front of a row of small bushes near our building. A plastic bag had blown into one of its branches, almost hidden from view. She walked over, gently unhooked it, folded it, and slipped it into her own bag. When I later told her I had seen this, she said ever so genuinely, 'I want to be someone who picks up the rubbish even when no one is looking.'

That simple sentence has stayed with me my entire life. It is the spirit behind so many Japanese manners that are easy to misunderstand, often perceived simply as 'politeness'. But when you observe closely, you begin to see what sits underneath them: a respect that is underscored by a deep sense of care and kindness towards others and our environment.

Let's take a look at how this manifests in daily life in Japan, through day-to-day gestures, shared spaces, interaction with nature and across generations. By looking into the 'why' behind these customs, we can start to see the value of humility appear.

RESPECT IN EVERYDAY GESTURES

In Japan, respect is often expressed through subtle actions. Bowing (*ojigi* お辞儀) is one of the most well-known examples. While many people think of it as a simple formality, it has long been shaped by Japan's religious and etiquette traditions, with the lowering of the head — considered the most vulnerable part of the body — expressing sincerity and non-aggression.

There are many forms of bows used for greetings, gratitude and apology, each with a different intention. Historically *reisansoku* (礼三息), meaning 'three breaths of bowing', described the length and sincerity of a bow. One inhales while lowering the upper body, exhales when the movement has finished, and inhales as one raises the upper body again. There is also the practice of leaving a pause after completing a bow to show whole-hearted intention.

Even now, if you walk into a shop, a restaurant or an office building in Japan, you will see small bows exchanged like silent ripples of acknowledgement – gestures that say, 'I recognize and see you'.

Even outside of formal settings, this sensitivity shows up in daily micro-gestures. Long after moving abroad, I still catch myself giving a slight head nod while on the phone. It is unconscious, yet it reflects a sincerity I cannot express with words alone.

Respect is also reflected through time. In Japan, punctuality is an expression of care. Arriving too early can disrupt someone's preparations; arriving late shows disregard for their time. To arrive at the promised moment is to say: *I honour your time.*

On public trains and buses in Japan, people rarely speak loudly, even in the most crowded ones during rush hour. Why is this the case? It is understood that each person contributes to the overall atmosphere. Playing music without headphones or speaking loudly on the phone is regarded as inconsiderate, not because of strict rules, but because it signals that one's own needs are being placed above everyone else's. In this sense, loudness becomes an expression of arrogance.

These gestures may seem small, but everyday actions reveal our values. When we can express acknowledgement and thoughtfulness, we remind ourselves, and each other, that we stand on equal footing.

RESPECT IN SHARED SPACES

Respect in Japan is not only interpersonal – it is also environmental. One of the things visitors often notice is how clean cities are, despite the lack of public rubbish bins. How can this be? It stems from a common understanding that if you create rubbish, you have the responsibility to dispose of it. Instead of littering or leaving it for someone else to handle, you see many people carrying a small bag so that they can take their litter home. Doing so encourages individuals to consider their impact on the world and take responsibility for what they bring into it.

Removing shoes when entering a home, traditional inn, temple or certain restaurants is another expression of shared respect. Shoes are placed neatly with the toes facing the exit, giving others enough space to get past them and allowing you to step into them easily when leaving. This practice reminds us that the spaces we enter do not belong solely to us – they are shared, and how we behave shapes the experience of those who come after us.

You also see this respect reflected in *onsen* (hot spring) customs, a wonderful, relaxing and rejuvenating experience loved by many. Before stepping into the water, everyone washes thoroughly to ensure the springs remain clean. Long hair is tied up and kept from touching the water; swimsuits and towels are not used in the hot springs; voices are kept soft so as not to disturb the calm atmosphere. The intention is clear: we look after the shared experience together.

Also, eating while walking is not a common practice in Japan. While this is partly because you don't want to make a mess on the street, it is also tied to the idea that food is best appreciated with care and attention, rather than while multitasking. Instead people find a bench or table, a quiet corner, or a designated space to enjoy their meal. Related to this practice is the custom of saying *itadakimasu* (いただきます) before each meal, often understood as

'I humbly receive'. This expression highlights gratitude not only for the food itself, but also for the people who prepared it and the natural resources that gifted us with this meal.

In all of these practices, a common theme comes to life: shared spaces are for everyone. They remind us that our needs do not take priority over the needs of others.

RESPECT ACROSS GENERATIONS

Respect for elders is another deeply rooted value in Japan. Every year on the third Monday of September, the country celebrates *Keirō no Hi* (敬老の日), Respect for the Aged Day, to honour the contributions, experiences and wisdom of older generations. This is not simply a ceremonial event, but reflects the everyday ways people make space for elders in conversation, offer seats on public transport, offer help with shopping bags or use specific respectful language when talking to them.

What stands out is that the intention behind this is not pity – it is reverence. It acknowledges the lives that came before us, the paths that were laid and the wisdom gained through time.

By recognizing the depth of experience of those who came before us, we honour our own greenness. When we respect older generations, we identify that we, too, are part of a larger story, with continued room to learn and grow.

RESPECT IN NATURE

Respect in Japan extends beyond people and spaces – it includes the natural world too. As mentioned in earlier chapters, nature is regarded not as something to control, but as something to honour. Humans are not the centre of the world; we are part of a larger whole. You see this in the fondness for forest bathing, in the mindful appreciation during hanami, and in the Shinto belief that mountains, trees, rivers and earth can all carry spiritual presence.

When we walk through a forest or take a hike, the intention is to avoid disturbing what already exists. When we experience the beauty of nature, it is important to recognize that we are not the protagonists of these moments but fortunate witnesses. These attitudes reflect a reverence for nature's impermanence and beauty.

As we look more deeply into ways respect is expressed in Japan, we realize that these customs extend far beyond etiquette – they are expressions of humility. Respect becomes the language through which we recognize one another, our environment and our community, ultimately creating space for genuine connection beyond our egos.

PRACTICE: COMING TO HUMILITY THROUGH RESPECT

This practice invites you to reconnect with the expressions of care you grew up with – the ones that shaped how you see the world, even if you no longer use them consciously. In returning to these subtle acts, we return to humility not as an idea, but as something lived.

STEP 1: A QUIET PAUSE

Find a comfortable place to sit.
Rest your hands gently where they naturally fall.
Take a slow breath in, and a long breath out.
You can close your eyes or keep them open –
whatever feels natural to you.

Let your heartbeat settle. Allow your pace to soften.

STEP 2: REMEMBERING YOUR EXPRESSIONS OF CARE

Think back to your childhood, either your home or the people who raised you. What were the small expressions of care you witnessed?
A warm hug, a comforting touch, a specific phrase, a habit of tidying the space before leaving, a moment of stillness before speaking, a way of offering help without being asked?
Stay with one expression that feels warm, familiar or grounding.

STEP 3: UNDERSTANDING THE THREAD BENEATH IT

Ask yourself softly:

- *What did this expression of care teach me?*
- *What did it make me feel?*
- *How did it remind me of my place in the world – not smaller, not bigger, but simply connected?*

Let your answers come to the surface at their own pace.

STEP 4: BRINGING IT BACK INTO YOUR LIFE

Now ask:

- *How might I bring this expression of care back, even just once this week?*
- *Who in my life could benefit from this small act of respect?*
- *How might this expression help me soften into humility?*

Choose one action – something small, sincere and achievable.

STEP 5: A CLOSING BREATH

Place one hand over your heart.
One slow inhale, one slow exhale.
Offer a simple internal acknowledgement:

May my expression of care reflect humility.
May my presence honour the people and spaces around me.
May my actions free me from any arrogance.
May I remember my place in the larger flow of things.

FINDING HUMILITY IN THE IN-YŌ 陰陽 BALANCE

To understand the essence of the sumomo – a blossom that carries meanings of independence and unpretentious elegance – I find it helpful to explore one more dimension of Japanese thought: the relationship between light and dark, seen and unseen, fullness and emptiness.

Although commonly known through the Chinese concept of Yin and Yang, this philosophy is also woven into Japanese culture, as *in-yō* (陰陽): *in* (陰) is the shadow, receptive, passive and *yō* (陽) is the light, active and expansive. This concept influences how we understand nature, the forces of the world and human wellbeing.

In-yō – the Japanese Understanding of Complementary Forces

In-yō teachings remind us that opposite forces are not in conflict. They coexist, depend on one another and continuously shift. Nothing in nature stays in one fixed state. The seasons change, the tides turn, our energy rises and falls. Importantly, in-yō does not assign moral value: the bright is not better than the dark, nor is the active superior to the passive. You can see this philosophy in Japanese martial arts such as *karate* (空手) and *aikidō* (合気道), recognizing that attack and defence are equally important, and that attention should be paid to the flow of forces.

In-yō is also reflected in traditional Japanese approaches to health. *Kanpō* (漢方), Japanese traditional herbal medicine, sees health as the dynamic balance between these two opposite forces. Illness is said to arise when this harmony is disrupted. Even today, kanpō is used in Japan's national healthcare system – a signal of how naturally this philosophy continues to shape daily life.

As we explore the sumomo's symbolism of inner confidence and self-understanding, in-yō invites us to explore the parts of ourselves that are not always visible. Just as nature reveals one face in daylight and another under moonlight, so too do we have qualities that unfold when no one is watching.

Japan and the Moon: Seeing Beauty in the Night

The daytime brings colour, activity, movement – the *yō* (陽) of nature. Yet when the sun sets, the world shifts. Something peaceful arises. A different kind of beauty appears – one that does not seek attention, yet expresses itself fully.

Perhaps this is why the Japanese relationship with the moon has endured for centuries. The moon carries its own calm presence and illuminates just enough for us to sense our surroundings, not dominate them.

Japanese poets, painters, musicians and monks have long turned to the moon for inspiration, recognizing in it an important element of our inner world.

The Japanese word for moon, *tsuki* (月), also means 'month', hinting at how the moon and the sense of time are closely intertwined. Japan once used a system called *wafū getsumei* (和風月名), which consisted of traditional month names based on the lunar calendar and seasonal rhythms.

Through these names you can see how communities interacted with nature's changes. A few examples and translations of traditional Japanese months help to illustrate this.

- ***Satsuki*** (皐月): the month for planting rice
- ***Nagatsuki*** (長月): the month when nights grow long
- ***Shimotsuki*** (霜月): the month when frost begins to appear

Even today, you can see these traditional months appear in poetry, art, festivals and everyday language, offering a reminder of our relationship with the natural world. When you pay attention, you start to notice how often *tsuki* appears in Japanese culture – in restaurant names, children's songs, product names, even in pop culture.

THE VOCABULARY OF THE MOON: THE ART OF EXPRESSING

One of the most beautiful examples of appreciating *in-yō* (陰陽) – the harmony of shadow and light – is the vast collection of *Yamato Kotoba* (大和言葉), native Japanese words that describe the moon in its many forms. There are dozens of them, but they do more than simply describe the moon, they reveal our relationship with it. Here is a selection of moon-appreciating words.

Words to Describe the Phases of the Moon:

- ***Tsuki-no-tsurugi*** (月の剣): The thin moon on the third night after a new moon, shaped like a sword.

- ***Izayoi*** (十六夜): The 16th night moon; a seemingly hesitant moon. Some even say that this slightly diminished moon is more elegant than a full moon, as it is not perfect.

- ***Tachimachizuki*** (立待月): The 17th night moon; the moon rising after one waits for it while standing.

- ***Imachizuki*** (居待月): The 18th night moon; the moon rising after one waits while seated.

- ***Nemachizuki*** (寝待月): The 19th night moon; the moon rising after one grows tired of waiting and has to lie down.

- ***Fukemachizuki*** (更待月): The 20th night moon; the moon appearing only after one wait for it deep into the night.

- ***Mochizuki*** (望月), ***eigetsu*** (盈月): Two of the many words used to describe the full moon, each carrying its own literary nuance.

Words to Describe the Appearance of the Moon:

- ***Oborozuki*** (朧月): A hazy spring moon.
- ***Tasogarezuki*** (黄昏月): A moon seen during twilight.
- ***Tsuki-suzushi*** (月涼し): The breezy feeling of seeing the moon during a summer night.
- ***Tsuki-itsuru*** (月凍つる): A winter night so cold it feels as though the moon itself might freeze.
- **Seigetsu** (霽月): The clear, bright moon after rain has cleared; also used to describe a clear, unclouded state of mind.
- ***Kogetsu*** (孤月): A solitary-looking moon that looks lonely.

Notice how these words describe not only the moon, but the human experience of waiting, watching, hoping, noticing and longing. They reflect a deep cultural attunement to stillness, patience and observation – qualities at the heart of humility. They also remind us that much of life happens in the shadows, in the quieter spaces of our inner world.

OTSUKIMI (お月見): THE ART OF MOON VIEWING

One cultural expression of this appreciation is *otsukimi* (お月見), the annual custom of honouring the full harvest moon. The festival typically takes place in autumn, on the 15th night of the 8th month of the traditional lunar calendar – a night said to have the year's most beautiful moon.

People offer seasonal foods such as *tsukimi-dango* (special rice dumplings), decorate with pampas grass and sit beneath the night sky to give thanks for the harvest. Along with these rituals, otsukimi represents a chance to observe the world not through the bright and active side, but through the night and quiet side. It invites us to reflect on the parts of ourselves that come alive when we are not performing or loud – the moods, emotions, dreams and questions that can only be heard when the world around us slows and quietens down.

In this way, otsukimi mirrors the inner work of humility: learning to sit with the dark and recognize it as part of our wholeness, of who we really are.

SHINGETSU (心月) – A HEART AS CLEAR AS THE MOON

This deep appreciation for the moon offers another layer of meaning for the sumomo. Just as the Japanese plum is often overlooked beside more famous blossoms, the moon's beauty emerges not from brightness but from its balance between presence and shadow.

In Japanese Buddhism, there is a word that captures this beautifully: *shingetsu* (心月). This term describes an enlightened heart, one as clear and bright as the moon, unclouded by ego.

The moon teaches us that our 'dark' sides – the passive, receptive and quieter parts – are not flaws. They are simply *in* – one half of *in-yō* (陰陽) – and are essential to who we are. They are part of the natural cycle of being human. They hold their own kind of beauty, depth and truth. And much like the sumomo fruit ripening in its own time, our inner confidence grows not from rejecting the dark but from learning to sit quietly within it.

This prepares us beautifully for the visualization to come – one that will guide you into the landscape of the night and help you honour the parts of yourself that the world, or even you, may not always see.

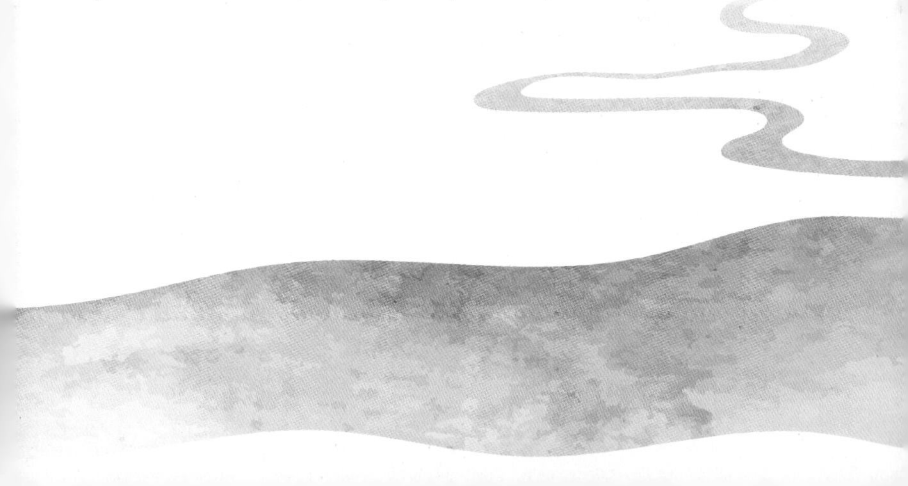

PRACTICE: MOON VISUALIZATION – EMBRACING THE SHADOW

This guided visualization invites you to welcome the quiet and look inwards, embracing the more passive, rounded and receptive sides of you, and is inspired by the luminous beauty of the moon in the dark sky.

THE VISUALIZATION

Find a quiet space. Sit or lie down comfortably. Slowly close your eyes and begin by focusing on your breath. Inhale slowly through your nose, filling your lungs with soothing ease. Exhale slowly through your mouth, releasing any tightness with kindness. Continue for a couple more breaths, allowing yourself to fully arrive in this moment and in your body.

Imagine you are surrounded by a vast night sky, lit up by a full moon. The air is fresh and crisp, your surroundings undisturbed, with the sounds of nature faintly keeping you company. The quietness and darkness are not frightening, but bring you a sense of ease and serenity.

Now, look up and you can see the full moon – round and glowing, offering a soft light. Not overly bright or strong as if to call attention to itself, but receptive and simply present.

As you take in the beauty of the night, lean in towards the sides of yourself that perhaps you have been ignoring or pushing away because you did not see them as active or expansive. Are there sides of yourself that are like the dark sky? Perhaps this is the side of yourself that longs for rest or calm. Or maybe this is the side that longs to slow down, be quiet or focus inwards.

Sit with this moment, just as the full moon watches over you without judgement. This is not a moment to criticize, analyse or overthink what comes to the surface. Simply observe.

Continue to take slow, intentional breaths. With each breath, imagine yourself acknowledging this *in* (陰) side of yourself. Allow yourself the gift of taking your time in this visualization.

The moment holds you and supports you as you begin to see your whole self with clarity.

Breathe in and welcome the sense of yourself strengthening.
Breathe out and feel yourself grounded in the growing confidence of knowing who you are.

Know that just as the moon continues to gift us with its grace every night, you too can remember to observe and embrace all aspects of yourself.

Take a few more breaths. Wiggle your fingers and toes softly, feeling your body present. When you feel ready, slowly open your eyes, carrying the elegance of the moon with you and understanding that when we embrace our shadows, we can embrace our whole selves with compassion.

CHAPTER WRAP-UP

As we close this chapter on Japanese plum blossoms, take a moment to notice whether the roots of a deeper, more grounded sense of your intrinsic self are growing. It may be the realization that you can incorporate some respectful actions into your life, or a renewed appreciation for parts of yourself you may have overlooked.

This chapter has been about turning your attention inwards and noticing how you move through the world: through humility, respect, the complementary forces that shape life and the lessons the moon offers us when we pay close attention to it. Remember that true confidence and humility do not come from external validation, but from how we choose to see ourselves. When these feelings become fragile, return to the practices and reflections in this chapter as reminders of your innate confidence – just as the sumomo blossom grows steadily, without seeking glory.

CHAPTER 5

LIVING OUBAITORI

LIVING *OUBAITORI*

As we reach the end of this journey together, we now bring together the wisdom of all four blossoms – sakura, ume, momo and sumomo. The key now is to integrate them into the rhythm of your life. Oubaitori is not something we practise only during peaceful seasons or moments of clarity. It is a way of living that accompanies us through joy, challenge, rest, growth, change and everything in between.

To live oubaitori is to live with intention.

It is to walk through the world appreciating each moment as precious, as the sakura blossoms taught us. It is to trust in our resilience and bloom even in challenging situations, just as the ume blossoms bravely flourish in the colder months. It is to live with childlike joy as the momo blossoms make their vibrant presence known. It is to have the quiet confidence in your unique unfolding as the sumomo blossoms humbly remind us.

We started this book by acknowledging the challenges of living in a world that can often feel like a constant comparison game, where we are urged to measure our worth against those around us. Now, as we wrap up, I hope that you recognize that your self-worth is not measured by comparison, speed or external markers, but by the inner alignment you cultivate with your most authentic self.

We are, and will continue to be, growing through the seasons of life. I encourage you to continue practising self-compassion and nurturing your authentic self.

YOUR OUBAITORI SEASONS

Living oubaitori is not about perfection or arriving at a final destination. It is about cultivating a way of being that honours the ebb and flow of life. Some days will feel like a full bloom; others may feel like early buds or fallen petals. All of this is part of the rhythm.

There will be seasons when you feel the sense of new beginnings – your sakura days.

There will be seasons when you must be brave and resilient – your ume days.

There will be seasons of playfulness and creativity – your momo days.

And there will be seasons of quieter confidence – your sumomo days.

All these phases are essential. All these versions of you belong.

When you embrace oubaitori as a way of living, you understand that you do not need to bloom at the same time as others. Your path is inherently yours, and the beauty of that truth will continue to unfold throughout your life.

YOUR OUBAITORI KOKORO (心)

Kokoro (心) is the Japanese word that encompasses heart, mind and spirit – the inner core where your truth lives. It unites our thoughts, emotions, essence, intentions and experiences. Rather than thinking of our mind and heart as separate, kokoro reminds us that our inner world is one interconnected space.

Take a moment to connect with your oubaitori kokoro – the heart of oubaitori. This is not simply your mind, but the deeper place within you that guides the rhythm of your blooming.

Here are some gentle questions to sit with:

- How am I respecting my own bloom?
- How can I align my actions and lifestyle with the way I wish to grow?
- How am I honouring my timing?
- What do I need to let go of to live in closer harmony with my oubaitori kokoro?
- Are there any thoughts or comparisons holding me back?

Your oubaitori kokoro is your vivid, most honest, colourful self. While we may look similar, none of us bloom in the same way. To live with your oubaitori kokoro is to make an active choice: a way of seeing the world differently. Where others may see blossoms as uniform shades of pink or white, you see, appreciate and celebrate each one's uniqueness.

This is not a wisdom reserved for a few people – it is something we can all access. And I believe we will all be better if we choose to nurture this way of seeing.

When you cultivate your oubaitori kokoro:

- You are kinder to nature, honouring its transient, unique beauty.
- You are kinder to others, celebrating their differences and individuality.
- And perhaps most importantly, you are kinder to yourself, recognizing that you are distinctly beautiful in every shade, in every season of your life.

AN INVITATION TO RETURN

My hope is that this book becomes a place to return to – whether as a guide to navigate transitions, a reminder of your strength in moments of doubt or a companion that helps you reclaim your joyful self.

May the wisdom of oubaitori inspire you to bloom authentically. And remember: your blossoming journey is uniquely yours, and this book will always be here for you to come back to when you need the tools to return to your true self.

May you find the time to continually lean in and look inwards throughout the evolving chapters of your life journey.

And above all, may these teachings help you come home to yourself, again and again.

Let us continue this blossoming journey with patience, compassion and trust – one season at a time.

A FINAL GUIDED REFLECTION: RETURNING HOME TO YOUR KOKORO (心)

This final practice is an invitation to come home – not to a place, but to yourself. Return home to your *kokoro* (心), the inner world where your heart, mind, spirit and essence exist. Think of this as a delicate way to close your journey through oubaitori, and a practice you can return to in any season of your life. A moment to reconnect with the wisdom that has been within you all along.

PREPARING THE SPACE

Find a comfortable place to sit or lie down.

You may wish to dim the lights or light a candle. You can also bring in some fresh air or fill your surroundings with a scent that brings you calm. That said, there is no need to create anything special or overcomplicate it – your presence is enough.

Rest your hands softly on your lap or alongside your body.
Let your shoulders drop.
Let your breath settle into whatever pace feels natural to you.

When you are ready, close your eyes.
Slowly inhale through your nose.
Then make a long, soft exhale through your mouth.
Repeat two to three times.

Allow your body to feel:
I am here.
I am safe.
I am home.

STEP 1: MEETING YOURSELF WHERE YOU ARE

Begin by noticing the quality of your inner world right now.
There is no need to change anything.
Just observe.

Notice any sensations in your body – the warmth, the heaviness, the stillness or the subtle movement of your breath.

Notice the emotions approaching beneath the surface – steady, gentle, complex or shifting.
Notice the thoughts passing by – quick, slow, loud, quiet, organized or scattered.
Everything is welcome here.

Again, we are not here to place judgement.
Simply observe whatever comes to the surface.

Imagine a small light close to your chest, illuminating your kokoro and bringing you a sense of comfortable warmth. As the light starts to fill you up, it starts to reveal the corners of your self you may have forgotten, ignored or brushed aside in the rush of daily life.

Let the light be warm.
Let it be kind.
Let it help you see and feel.

STEP 2: RETURNING TO YOUR NATURAL RHYTHM

Now imagine your kokoro as a small garden – uniquely yours.

A place where all four blossoms of oubaitori grow in their own time. Notice what is blooming right now.

Are you in a sakura moment – seeing beauty in the present or feeling a new beginning?
Are you in an ume moment – finding strength in difficulty?
Are you in a momo moment – reconnecting with joy and playfulness?
Are you in a sumomo moment – feeling quietly confident, or learning to trust your pace?

There is no right answer.
Every blossom carries its own wisdom.

Let yourself recognize the season you are in – without judgement, without comparison.
Gently acknowledge where you are with the mantra:
I am exactly where I need to be.

STEP 3: LISTENING TO YOUR KOKORO

Ask your kokoro softly:

- What are you longing for right now?
- How can I align my actions with what you are hoping for?
- Is there something I have been avoiding that wants to be seen?
- Is there something I have been holding too tightly that wants to be released?

Do not force answers to appear. Let them come the way blossoms do – gradually, and in their own time.

You may not have answers to all these questions, and that is okay.
Even a whisper is enough.
Even a feeling is enough.
Whatever comes to the surface, meet it with compassion.
Meet it with patience. Meet it with gratitude.

Let your kokoro know that you are finally listening.

STEP 4: RELEASING WHAT NO LONGER BELONGS

Now, imagine exhaling the things that weigh on your kokoro –
the comparisons, expectations and narratives that no longer serve you.

With each exhale, let something soften. Let something loosen.
Let something gently fall away, lightening your load.

And with each inhale, imagine receiving what nourishes you – spaciousness, clarity, kindness, steadiness.

Slowly, breath by breath, create room within yourself to bloom again.

STEP 5: COMING HOME TO YOURSELF

Place one hand over your heart and one over your lower belly, feeling your kokoro as a connecting force.

Let this be a moment of recognition:
Here I am.

As a complex, evolving, imperfect, beautiful human.
As someone who does not need to rush, compare or justify their timing.
As someone who blooms in their own season.
As someone who trusts the wisdom of their kokoro.

Take one final slow breath – filling your kokoro with light.
When you're ready, gently open your eyes.

A CLOSING THOUGHT

You can come back to this practice whenever you feel overwhelmed, unanchored, disconnected or in need of deeper grounding.

Your kokoro is always here.
Your season is ever evolving.
Your blossoming is a lifelong journey.
And you always have the power to come back home.

AUTHOR'S NOTE: WHY I NEEDED THIS BOOK TOO

There is an underlying truth beneath every book, and I want to share mine with you.

I did not write *Oubaitori* because I consider myself a master of this wisdom. As I shared in the introduction, I, too, found myself measuring my self-worth constantly against others for many years. I chased versions of myself that I thought would make me worthy – believing that if I were more beautiful, slimmer, more social, more successful, more like 'that person', I would finally be able to feel at ease with myself.

During this time, my wellbeing was poor. I knew I was in a constant state of anxiety and unease, trying to hold myself together while acting as if everything was 'great'. It was in these cycles of comparison that I found myself reconnecting with my Japanese roots. This happened during the global coronavirus pandemic. While this was a devastating time, it forced me to slow down for the first time in many years. I was back in Japan as an adult for an extended period of time, something I had not done since my teenage years. During these days, I slowly began to notice the teachings and concepts I had grown up with but had brushed off: in the quiet moments with myself, in interactions with others, and in the serenity of nature. I was coming back home to myself.

The lessons and concepts that are woven into oubaitori come from this sense of longing. After these learnings had helped me find a sense of ease in myself, I started to wonder. Perhaps these were concepts and ways of approaching life that could be beneficial to others? What if we began to do the opposite of what seems to be the trend in society – what if we slowed down, reconnected with joy and our energy, spent time in nature and found the power of respecting others? The work I do now stems from the belief that these teachings can meaningfully support our holistic wellbeing and how we see ourselves and the world.

Now, do I have everything figured out? Absolutely not.

I am sure there will be days when I compare myself to others in some shape or form. Perhaps that is part of human nature, as we are social creatures. However, if and when that happens, I intend to come back to this book myself, to reflect on the wisdom of oubaitori, and continue to remind myself of my own unique timing and presence. As a forever student of myself and life, I hope to continue growing and learning to be the most authentic version of myself at every stage of my journey.

Writing this book was part of my continued journey.

It helped me slow down.

It helped me honour my timing.
It helped me see my own life with more kindness.
And it helped me return to the parts of myself I had ignored for far too long.

If this book has resonated with you – even through a single sentence, a practice or a moment of reflection – then I am grateful. It means that the wisdom of oubaitori has travelled beyond me and continued its journey through you.

We live in a world that often asks us to be louder, faster, more productive and more perfect. But the blossoms remind us that growth can be quiet, authentic, messy, beautiful and entirely our own. You do not need to bloom like anyone else. You simply need to bloom as you.

BLOSSOM SITES IN JAPAN

MAP LOCATIONS:

CHERRY BLOSSOM SITES

1 Takada Castle Site Park (高田城址公園), Jōetsu City, Niigata

2 Mount Yoshino (吉野山), Yoshino Town, Nara

3 Philosopher's Path (哲学の道), Kyoto City, Kyoto

4 Hirosaki Castle (弘前城), Hirosaki City, Aomori

5 Miharu Taki-zakura (三春滝桜), Miharu Town, Fukushima Prefecture

6 Yamataka Jindai-zakura (山高神代桜), Hokuto City, Yamanashi Prefecture

7 Usuzumi-zakura (淡墨桜), Motosu City, Gifu Prefecture

JAPANESE APRICOT BLOSSOM SITES

8 Atami Ume Garden (熱海梅園), Atami City, Shizuoka Prefecture

9 Tanigawa Ume Grove (谷川梅林), Tachibana Town, Fukuoka Prefecture

10 Anou Ume Grove (賀名生梅林), Gojo City, Nara Prefecture

11 Nanaore Ume Garden (七折梅園), Tobe Town, Ehime Prefecture

12 Kairakuen Garden (偕楽園), Mito City, Ibaraki Prefecture

13 Soga Ume Grove (曽我梅林), Odawara City, Kanagawa Prefecture

14 Ogose Ume Grove (越生梅林), Ogose Town, Saitama Prefecture

PEACH BLOSSOM SITES

15 Fuefuki Peach Blossom Utopia (笛吹桃源郷), Fuefuki City, Yamanashi Prefecture

16 Hanamomo no Sato (花桃の里), Achi Village, Nagano Prefecture

17 Gōdo Station Hanamomo (神戸駅花桃), Midori City, Gunma Prefecture

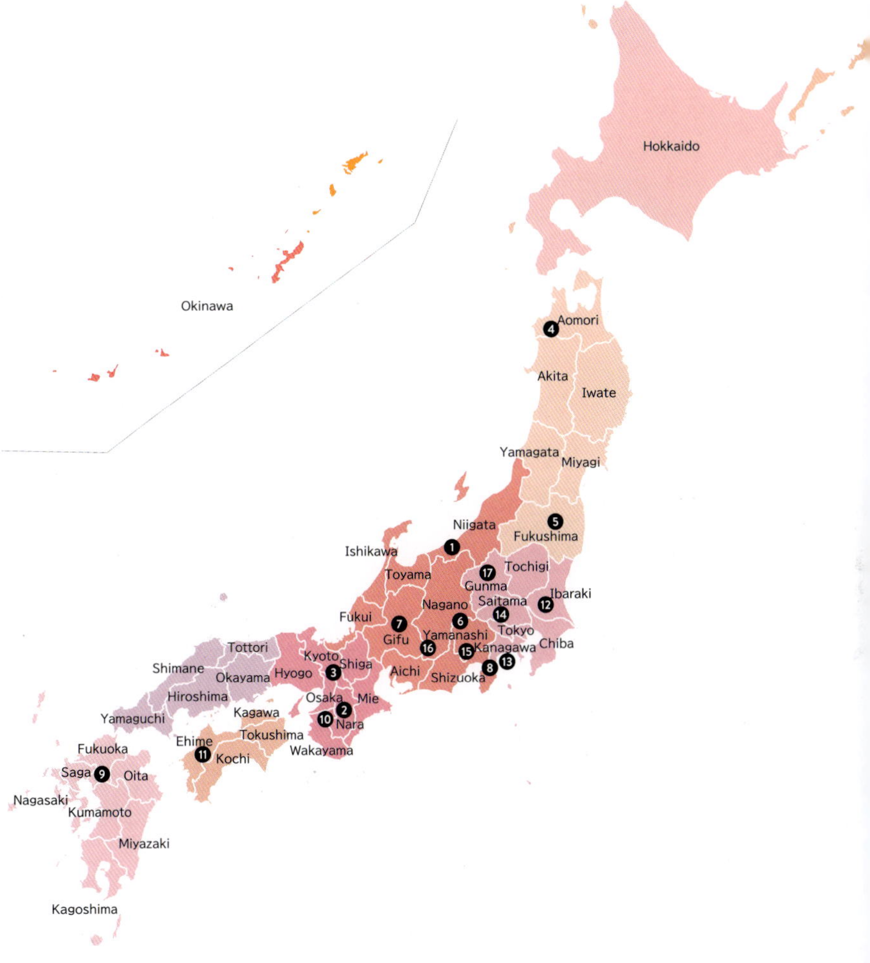

BLOSSOM SITES IN JAPAN

INDEX

ABOUT THE AUTHOR

Saori Okada is a writer and the founder of Mogami® 最上 Wellness, where she brings a culturally grounded perspective to Japanese holistic wellbeing rooted in tradition and lived experience, offering 1:1 coaching, corporate wellbeing programmes, public speaking and immersive group experiences. Born and raised in Japan, and now based in London, her work is shaped by a life lived both within Japan and abroad.

A lifelong student of Japanese calligraphy and with more than 25 years of practice under her calligraphy name 星洗 (*Seisen*), Saori draws deeply from Japan's artistic and philosophical heritage. Her roots remain central to her understanding of purpose, wellbeing and the discipline of returning to one's own path.

Before founding Mogami, Saori spent more than seven years working in marketing and media analytics in New York and Toronto. Through her work now, she shares Japanese wisdom with care, clarity and cultural integrity, informed by her background as a registered health coach and her international experience. She has worked with clients in the UK and internationally, including YouTube, Meta, Mazda and Carter Jonas.

www.mogamiwellness.com
@mogami_wellness

ACKNOWLEDGEMENTS

I would like to thank my parents, who gave me the gift of encouraging me to be nothing other than myself throughout my life, and who instilled in me the belief to trust my own path. Thank you to my sister, Reiko, for her kind and patient soul, and for letting me follow along while growing up – you taught me, without ever saying it, that there is room to grow in one's own way.

Thank you to my husband, Benjamin, for loving and empowering me as I am, and for reminding me that it is the everyday moments that give life its meaning. And thank you to our precious daughter, with whom I now begin a new chapter – one that will bloom in its own, vibrant way.

To my dear friends, who have walked alongside me throughout my life – thank you for amplifying moments of joy and sitting with me through the more difficult ones. You know who you are.

And finally, to my editor, Louisa, thank you for the opportunity to write this book, and thanks too to the team at Hachette, for their care in bringing it into the world.